ALONE

FINDING CONNECTION IN A LONELY WORLD

ANDY BRANER

TH1NK, an
Imprint of
NavPress

NavPress is the publishing ministry of The Navigators, an international Christian organization and leader in personal spiritual development. NavPress is committed to helping people grow spiritually and enjoy lives of meaning and hope through personal and group resources that are biblically rooted, culturally relevant, and highly practical.

For a free catalog go to www.NavPress.com
or call 1.800.366.7788 in the United States or 1.800.839.4769 in Canada.

ISBN-13: 978-1-61747-992-2

Cover design by Arvid Wallen

Some of the anecdotal illustrations in this book are true to life and are included with the permission of the persons involved. All other illustrations are composites of real situations, and any resemblance to people living or dead is coincidental.

Braner, Andy.
Alone : finding connection in a lonely world / Andy Braner.
p. cm.
Includes bibliographical references.
ISBN 978-1-61747-992-2
1. Loneliness--Religious aspects--Christianity. I. Title.
BV4911.B73 2012
248.8'3--dc23
2012020005

Printed in the United States of America

2 3 4 5 6 7 8 / 17 16 15 14 13

"*Alone* is a fantastic book. Andy has his heart on the pulse of this generation and I thank him for an honest, insightful, and heartfelt response to the loneliness that plagues young people today. I wish every young person would read this book."

—SEAN McDOWELL, educator; speaker; author of *Apologetics for a New Generation*

"I remember a teacher having us study the problem of 'alienation,' by which she meant the severing of people from the structures of meaning in society. Technology was supposed to solve that problem and bring people together. To our shock, though, the very tools that were to bring us together are actually driving us apart. Andy is just the guy to make the case, and the timing is perfect. We have an opportunity to rebuild biblical community for the sake of the gospel and for the souls of those in the rising generation, and we must seize it."

—JEFF MYERS, PhD, president, Summit Ministries

"Andy Braner's commitment to teenagers is extraordinary. Through Camp KIVU, his writing, and his various outreach programs, Andy has shown how one man can make a difference in the lives of young people."

—TORRE KNOS, producer, *Abel's Field*

"Don't just check it out—buy this book. Andy understands teenagers better than anyone else I know, and that's saying a lot. Loneliness is the primary issue kids face today."

—RYAN DOBSON, co-host of Dr. James Dobson's Family Talk radio program; founder, KOR Ministries

"Andy Braner is one of the most effective communicators I have ever met. He has the ability to connect with, challenge, and persuade a wide variety of audiences. He works, writes, and educates tirelessly to accomplish the goal of godly authenticity."

—JOEY MOORECRAFT, dean, Students Fellowship Christian School, Roswell, Georgia

"Andy speaks the truth of life. He is a man of hope in a chaotic, lonely, ever-changing world. No one speaks with creative clarity to the issues of the day like Andy. Read every word of this book, as I have, and you will find that it's an extremely important and needed book."

—WES ROBERTS, leadership mentor, Leadership Design Group

"This book explores the great paradox students face today: how they can be so connected and yet so lonely; how they can have hundreds of Facebook friends but no real ones; how they can be glued to their phones and feel that no one is listening. Andy gets to the heart of the matter—knowing what it means to be made in the image of the relational God. If you are student or young adult or one who mentors any, this is must-reading."

—JOHN STONESTREET, speaker and author for Breakpoint and Summit Ministries

"Andy Braner has written a book that nails a problematic issue of this generation: aloneness. God created us to be together, truly together, but severe loneliness has hurt so many of our youth. Andy provides solid answers backed with real-life stories that will inspire you to hope again."

—CARL MEDEARIS, writer and speaker

CONTENTS

INTRODUCTION

I'VE BEEN WORKING with teenagers for the past fifteen years of my professional life. I've pastored, befriended, counseled, and had a lot of fun with the craziest demographic on the planet: *you!* We've had lock-ins, camping trips, short-term mission excursions, and all sorts of programs. It's been a blast. But, as you probably could have guessed, it hasn't been all fun and games.

I've helped students understand divorce.

I've walked with them through major addictions.

I've talked them down from suicide.

I've been privy to some serious sexual deviances they wouldn't share with the most secretive of priests.

And I've heard their hearts.

When people ask me, "What's the biggest problem we can identify in the teenage nation today?" it's an easy answer: Teenagers are living all alone!

Now, hear me out. I know that sounds a bit strange; you are probably the most connected generation in history. Still, Facebook was started not long ago in 2004, YouTube has been around since only the early part of the twenty-first century, and I remember when e-mail first started. (Yes. I do.)

It came to the university while I was there! I was sitting in my dorm room at Baylor University when my roommate came running down the hallway and burst into my room.

"You'll never guess what I just did!" He was gasping for breath. "I just talked over the computer with someone in India."

At that moment, I knew the world was getting smaller.

Even though we have witnessed a modern-day miracle of connection, I stand by my story: Most teenagers *are* walking through life alone, and *that* is the source of so many of the traditional ills we often witness within the teen nation.

They have no one to turn to, no one to count on, no one who is going to be there, and no one who understands them. (At least they *feel* that way.)

Don't believe me?

Ask the students at your school.

Ask them who they feel they can trust, no matter what.

Ask them who they go to when they feel down.

Ask them how they plan on coping with the next tragedy.

Ask them.

Ask them, and you'll find a generation hopeless for the future. They have the energy to change the world, but they don't have the emotional stamina to make it through the week. Parents often ask, "How can I get my kid off the video-gaming system?" And I want to ask, "Why do you think they're on that video-game system?"

See, I believe that teens—your friends, maybe even you—are wanting *some* control in their lives, and it just so happens that Xbox, PlayStation, and the Wii offer them just that. I've watched students who connect with people all over the world while they play World of Warcraft. I've seen college students find community when they play Call of Duty. While they are connecting with people, the sense of *truly* belonging, well, it's just not the same.

It's not the same to talk to someone in Germany about a video game.

It's not the same to limit one's secret comments to 140 characters on Twitter.

And even though Facebook gives us the ability to build a convenient corner of lives over the vast Web interface, the light of a computer screen isn't bright enough to shine deep into our hearts and souls.

We need real people.

We need somewhere to cry out when life doesn't make sense.

We need friends to rejoice when we rejoice.

We need a place to mourn together.

We need somewhere to explore issues we don't feel safe exploring alone.

How many times have you seen someone rushing to see if anyone had posted on their latest story, update, or photo album? We find safety in our tribes, wherever they may be. We find peace where we know the parameters. We've learned from the best of them (our parents, our youth leaders) how to avoid situations that create conflict, and we've created places where there is an illusion of community.

But if technological connections are the only ones we make, then we're missing something.

We're missing what it means to rejoice in times of celebration.

We're missing the joy in the eyes of a friend who approves.

We don't know how to sit in the quiet of tragedy with someone else.

We're missing the comfort of tears streaming down a friend's face because he's sad for you.

When we fail to share experiences, which are becoming fewer and fewer, there is a loss of meaning in life. And many of us—especially young people, already searching for purpose—are starting to ask the question "Is this all there is?"

Sure, youth leaders like me can play the blame game and point fingers at the parents, teachers, mentors, and friends. Some want to blame culture as a whole, but I'm not into pointing fingers. I try to see the situation for what it is.

It's easy to be an armchair quarterback and blame Hollywood.

We can start vilifying Facebook and Twitter, but in all reality, those are great networks that help keep people in touch.

We can form all kinds of youth ministry dedicated to reducing drug use, sexual relationships, and transformative culture, but until we begin working diligently to create environments where teens can connect spiritually and emotionally, we're wasting our time.

I know this.

That's why I'm writing this book. To you. To the teenage population. Because the more important question is "How can we solve it?" How can *we* help *you* to develop into men and women who are *whole*, *fully* connected, and *fully* purposed?

Although this book is written for just the teen crowd, know that you're not the only ones struggling. As I travel, I've also found many college students, parents, and professionals who are dealing with the same feelings. They're walking through life all alone, looking for the next something to fill the tank, but they're only winding up empty, hopeless, and alone.

I've seen mothers crying, fathers wandering, and friends trying to conjure up help to connect with someone else. All of them are walking through life acting as though everything is okay, but the reality of the situation is that they're just sad. If you could peel back the masks they wear on their faces like the layers of an onion, it doesn't take too many layers to get down to the tender pain.

They're asking questions like:

Is this how life is supposed to turn out?

Am I fulfilling my purpose?

Is this all there is?

Do we fill our minds with helpful God stories just to make us feel good? Or is there something to this faith?

When I follow Jesus, is there something that serves a far broader purpose than simply saying a prayer, singing a song, or praying over a meal?

My hope in writing this book is to gather all of us who are walking through life as though it all depends on us. If we can circle the wagons and recognize there are other people out there feeling just the way we are, there might be a chance for finding a community of people who really care.

In fact, I know there is.

I've seen it.

I've lived it.

I know it!

As a matter of core theology, I know there are people in the world put there as fellow sojourners. I know God created mankind, not as individuals destined to walk alone but for fellowship together. When we live *with* each other rather than *at* each other, we can find a beautiful harmony of existence with one another.

If you think reading this book is going to solve all your problems, you're mistaken. But maybe, just maybe, there are going to be some stories you can identify with here that will help you see that you're not the only one—you're not *alone*—and sometimes that's all it takes to start moving forward.

I believe in the Bible.

I believe in good and evil.

I believe in God, and I believe in an evil adversary.

I believe the adversary has done an impeccable job of splitting up the power of like-minded people into their own shadows of loneliness in the world. He has isolated us into the corner of insignificance to keep us from experiencing the abundant life Jesus came to proclaim.

The time has come to end this nonsense.

We are called to a higher place.

We are called to a higher purpose.

For it's only in our unity that we can find the power God meant to give us to help in restoring the world.

Come, join me in trying to figure out why we're feeling so alone. My hope is that in doing so, you can begin to create meaningful communities right where you are. It might be that kid sitting across from you in the cafeteria. It may be that you need to reach out to a coworker. There could be someone in your life right now feeling the same feelings of loneliness, and together you can find what Jesus really meant when He said, "Where two or three gather in my name, there am I with them" (Matthew 18:20).

Aristotle once said, "Friendship is a single soul dwelling in two bodies." And the feeling of friendship is more valuable than all the riches in the world.

This isn't meant to be a self-help book.

It's not even really supposed to be an evangelical tool.

My only purpose in writing this book is to expose the feelings that we drive deeply into our souls, the feelings that keep us from truly living. My hope is that we can tackle the reasons so many of us feel alone in the world and shine some light on how to make loneliness disappear.

You don't have to be alone anymore.

CHAPTER 1

ALONE

It is not good for the man to be alone.

— Genesis 2:18

I just don't belong . . . anywhere.

— Buddy, *Elf*

EVERY CHRISTMAS, IT'S a Braner family tradition to dial in TBS to the twenty-four-hour *Elf* marathon. There's apparently an executive at TBS who thinks *Elf* should be played nonstop, for days on end, around the Christmas holidays, and I think he or she needs a raise.

Elf, of course, is the story of Buddy (played by Will Ferrell), a human who was accidentally brought back to the North Pole one year when Santa returned from his global gift distribution. While Santa had been checking out the cookies, Buddy (a non-elf baby) had crawled into his sack. Now the North Pole had a problem on its hands.

What were they supposed to do with this little baby?

Which house did he come from?

Seeing the return trip as an improbable solution, they adopt Buddy, who lives with Papa Elf.

Soon Buddy grows taller than everyone around him.

Buddy is heavier than every elf in the community.

His fingers are too big to put the Etch A Sketch knobs on right.

While he wants to fit in, while he wants to contribute to his community, Buddy just wasn't made to be an elf. So after a talk with Papa Elf, Buddy sets out to find a place where he fits in by seeking out his father in New York City.

But you know what happens: A grown man who dresses as an elf and eats maple syrup on everything doesn't fit in very well in New York, either.

He doesn't fit in at the North Pole as a human.

He doesn't fit in with the high-rise society of New York.

Buddy the Elf looks into the camera and says, "I just don't belong . . . anywhere."

Anywhere?

Have you ever felt like that?

Have you ever felt that you just don't belong?

You try to perform in your athletics, but it seems that at every turn you fail.

You study as hard as you can, but in the end you only get Bs.

You find making friends harder than just staying at home and holing up in your room. *At least no one can make fun of me here*, you think.

I think you'd be surprised if you polled your friends walking through the hallways of today's schools. Sure, they laugh out loud, they talk on their cell phones, they seem to have purpose on the outside, but I wonder how many of them would look into life's camera like Buddy and admit, "I just don't belong . . . anywhere."

I'm blessed to have traveled the world working with people of all nationalities. I started at a summer camp for teens in Colorado and made it my mission to help people who think they don't belong anywhere to connect.

I've worked in the church with teens just like you.

I've worked in small groups.

I've been a part of youth conferences spanning the globe.

My point is, I talk with teenagers from all over, and one thing I'm finding out is there are more of you out there than you think.

I've got stacks of letters on my desk (yes, the paper kind) telling about how even the most popular kids in the school are finding it harder and harder to connect with friends.

"I just made the cheer team, but I still don't fit in."

"I just got accepted to college, and even though my parents are happy, I'm not sure that I am."

"I'm dating this girl, and I think she might be the one, but she has no idea who I really am."

One particular letter I read recently was from a quarterback on the high school varsity football team. He's pretty successful. Parents all know who he is. He has access to as many friends as he could ever want. But one statement jumped off the page: "How can I get to a point where I'm not so *alone*? I just don't belong here."

Can you imagine?

Can you imagine being successful and recognized but still feeling all alone inside?

I spend a fair amount of time talking to youth ministers, pastors, and parents trying to develop teen-friendly programs in the church environment. They're all wanting to know how they can beat the local teen issues.

"Andy, how can we address sexuality in a relevant way?"

"How can we keep kids from going out and smoking weed?"

"There's just nothing to do in our town, so our kids are out drinking and partying. Is there any curriculum you have to help?"

You know as well as I do . . .

It's not about sex.

It's not about drugs.

It's not about alcohol.

It's not about addiction.

The number one issue at the core of all humanity lies in our own belonging. We just don't feel as though we fit in. We're walking through life looking for people to connect with, but often the connection seems superficial and lacks any deep understanding. Sure, we have friends, but how many friends would really drop anything they're doing to help us?

You've found a community through your sexual activity.

You've sought friends that will gather around and light up with you.

You've even found people who find it intriguing to go out and get drunk together.

Because, for a time, you can put aside feeling like you don't matter, and you can matter to someone.

But if you're honest with yourself . . .

When you close the door at night and think about all the people you know and, just as important, when you think about all the people who know *you*, are you able to come up with a list of people who carry the ever-important role of caring for you?

When you walk the streets of your town, do you feel like Buddy?

Do you feel like you don't belong . . . anywhere?

Loneliness is the root cause of sexual promiscuity as more and more teens look for someone, anyone, to reach out and love them in any way. Hollywood tells us that if only we can hook up with someone, we might be able to find love.

Loneliness is the root cause of many introductions to alcoholism. Nobody begins to drink by themselves. Most of the time, early-drinking stories are about being with friends, hanging out, being conditioned that the bottle equals a social interaction that will fill that empty spot in your soul. But if you really consider the friends you make when you're out partying, do you really think they would be there for you if the alcohol were taken away?

Addictions can be where we find security. Whether it's the drugs you use or even the foods you eat, when you find an addiction in your life, it usually has to do with the desire for some kind of control. Your life might be spinning out of control, so you find a substance to at least know there is something you can count on.

But in the end, addiction leads to only more addiction. We never learn how to stand up and say, "It's enough."

Eating out of control leads only to a need for more tomorrow.

Hooking up with a boyfriend or girlfriend lasts for the moment, and then the process of being alone starts all over again and you need more.

Weed today leads only to more weed tomorrow, and maybe something stronger the next day.

Loneliness and the attempt to fill the emptiness in our hearts is causing an epidemic of depression, and, if not treated early, it could result in a young adult spinning out of control in what many of my colleagues call "the messy twenties."

GOD'S DESIGN

It's no secret that God designed us to be more than just robots on this planet.

He gave us a sense of love, honor, and respect.

He created majestic mountain ranges for us to marvel.

He stopped the seas at just the right spot where we can look out and wonder.

He fashioned the small and the large so we might discover His handiwork.

In fact, the Bible says, "The heavens declare the glory of God; the skies proclaim the work of his hands" (Psalm 19:1). It is right to presume He meant for us to live for more.

As God was in the business of creating the mighty oceans and the majestic mountains, we see in the Creation story a special mark for the creation of mankind.

Genesis 1:26 says, "Let us make mankind in our image, in our likeness, so that they may rule over the fish in the sea and the birds in the sky, over the livestock and all the wild animals, and over all the creatures that move along the ground." It was a moment where everything stopped to focus on man. Can you imagine what the heavenly beings must have thought when God breathed life into humanity?

Mortal.

Designed to live in the affects of glory, yet destined to live in a world of sin.

God's most clever creative relationship would be at the first breath Adam took.

God made this relationship special.

He walked with mankind.

He talked with mankind.

He gave over the management of *all* creation to this new being.

What must it have been like to be an angel? One day your best friends are immortal beings who can fly with wings, fight with supernatural force, and live forever. Then the next day, mortal man appears on the scene. Created in God's image.

When we get to verse 26, I wonder, *If I'm made in God's image, does that mean I look like God?* I suppose because there are so many humans on the planet who look nothing alike, the image of God must span more than the stubbly beard I can grow when it gets cold. Surely the image of God is bigger than the color of our hair or the hue of our eyes.

So it must mean God created me with intrinsic characteristics He models from the beginning:

Love.

Compassion.

Creativity.

Hope.

The ability to make things.

A sense of right and wrong.

A need for communion.

The angels must have been like kids in the candy store. "What has God created today?" And then they saw Adam walking through the garden.

But Adam wasn't alone in the garden. God already made the animals to walk with him, but He hadn't named them yet. He called Adam to the table and asked him to begin the process of naming the animals one by one.

Can you imagine what it was like on that day?

I've often wanted to see a creative team make the *Adam Names the Animals* movie. I can kind of see it like this:

Garden of Eden, Pool of Tranquility — Sunrise

ADAM wakes to a magical sunrise, stretches his arms high to the sky, and begins touring the daily duties of management. He checks the fruit and vegetables and spends time waiting for God to show up by the pool of tranquility.

GOD: Adam, where are you?

ADAM: Just hanging out here by the pool.

GOD: Oh, I thought I might find you here. Adam, I have a special job for you today.

ADAM: Sounds great. What's up?

GOD: Today you're going to make history. I need you to meet me by the big oak tree, south of the apple orchards, and I'll bring all the animals to you.

ADAM: Thanks, God, but I can just—

GOD: Wait till I'm finished.

(*Adam sits in silence with respect as the thunder rolls around him.*)

GOD: I need you to give them all names—not the kind of names that will be proper names but rather what they will be called *forever*!

ADAM: That's a great idea, God. In fact, I was just thinking of a name the other day for that big fish I saw in the ocean. Check this out: beluga whale!

(*All heavenly beings roll their eyes at God.*)

MICHAEL: (*whispering*) Are you kidding me? Beluga whale? That's the best he can do?

GOD: Don't worry, Michael. I'm going to have a lot of different languages in the future. We'll change it when Spanish comes along. (*Pauses*) Man should not be alone.

Excuse me?
Angels were in the garden.
God was in the garden.
Adam was in the garden.

Animals were in the garden.

And God decides out of nowhere to declare the detriment of loneliness in all mankind?

From a distance, it seems like Adam had plenty of relationships going for him. He had dogs to play with, birds to watch, and fish to catch. He even had God chatting with him. But for some reason, God saw it beneficial to point out Adam's aloneness right there in the beginning.

Why is that?

I've read this section in Genesis a million times before, but I've always skipped right over the statement "It is not good for the man to be alone" (2:18). It's almost like a foreshadowing of what we know is coming. Of course, Eve is just around the corner, so God needed to say that, right?

But what if God is also proclaiming a fundamental truth of humanity through this seemingly trite statement with Adam in the garden? What if He's actually telling the generations to come, "Watch out! It's not good for you to hang out with just animals and the supernatural"? Or what if He's trying to tell the future believers, "There's more to life than simply walking and talking with Me"?

Now, don't get all bent out of shape here. God most certainly wants to have a relationship with us. The Great Commandment starts with "Love the Lord your God with all your heart and with all your soul and with all your mind" (Matthew 22:37). So in no way am I trying to diminish the value of a relationship between God and mankind.

But what if there's more?

What if the second part of the Great Commandment has equal value to the first? Jesus said, "And the second is like it: 'Love your neighbor as yourself.'" Then He adds, "All the Law and the Prophets hang on these two commandments" (verses 39-40).

Ha!

Can you see it?

Adam walked with God!

Adam talked with God!

He ate next to the Creator.

He shared joy.

He had pure relationship. They were at each other's beck and call. It must have been a wonderful union. But it was God who declared that man needed something more.

The early manuscripts say, "I will make a helper suitable for him" (Genesis 2:18).

A suitable helper?

Wasn't God suitable enough?

Didn't God have enough relationship to look after Adam's needs?

He takes care of the whole universe, or, as the children's song declares, "He's got the whole world in His hands," but He doesn't have enough for Adam?

Well, maybe it wasn't God's deficiency.

Maybe God created Adam to be needy.

Maybe Adam's relationship with God was not built in fullness but contained a hole God created inside of humanity so we might recognize the importance of each other.

It was (and is) *brilliant.*

It's a theological mystery to try to explain relationship as God intended. Sure, we can make feeble attempts to answer why God created man and why He created woman. We can try to explain God's intention for us to be His worship team here on the planet, but, lest you forget, God was already well praised in the heavens. Isaiah 6 speaks of the angels who crowded around God's throne singing, "Holy, holy, holy is the LORD Almighty" (verse 3). It's not as though God really needed us to praise Him, like a star with his posse following him to the world premiere of his next movie.

No, I don't think God created mankind just for Himself.

It might seem as though God would create mankind as a toy—a creation He could manage as though He didn't have anything else to do.

But why would God waste time creating mankind to play the silly games of life?

Doesn't God have enough to do as He manages the universe?

I think there's a third way of looking at this Creation story. I wonder if God's creation of mankind wasn't a dim reality of the relationship He exists in already. John 1:1 says, "In the beginning was the Word, and the Word was with God, and the Word was God." Verse 14 goes on to say, "The Word became flesh and made his dwelling among us." And most theologians would agree that the "Word" John speaks of is actually Jesus, God incarnate, with all the fullness of deity dwelling in Himself. Isn't it interesting that "in the beginning" there was already this relationship coexisting in the seemingly oneness of God?

It's noteworthy to look at Genesis 1:26. It doesn't say, "Let *me* make mankind in *my* image." Rather, God chooses to use the plural pronouns, "Let *us* make mankind in *our* image, in *our* likeness" (emphasis added). It's almost as if God created mankind as a mirror image of the relationship He has with Himself. It's a delicate dance of giving and serving as they (the Father, the Son, and the Spirit) work together in cognition to love and be loved in perfect harmony.

Adam's problem wasn't his longing for sexuality or his discovery that all the animals were able to mate. No, the turmoil in Adam's existence prior to Eve was centered around the obvious relationship God models to the universe as a perfect union.

In other words, Adam was alone.

He didn't fit in . . . *anywhere.*

He didn't have anyone to share the naming of the animals or the managing of the plants with. He was primarily concerned with his own needs and, in the self-centeredness of the original creation, found himself unable to fit into any other part of society.

So this is the gaping hole in the human condition: to know someone else and be known by someone else, to have the ability to give and receive in constant relationship.

Yes, God wants us to love Him from every fiber of our being, but He also wants us to lean on each other.

It's not the secret fulfillment that may come from a drug binge, a sexual desire, or a shopping addiction.

And it doesn't mean we have to be constantly dating or on our way to marriage.

What it does mean is we must be honest about our needs and begin to meet needs of someone else. From the very start of life, a baby needs a mother, a toddler needs socialization, an elementary student needs to fit in. And by the time you reach adolescence, you need a strong support group around you. It might be your family, it may be your friends, it might be your neighborhood, it may be your community, but you need a place to fit in and be validated.

I don't think it was an accident when Jesus said, "A new command I give you: Love one another. As I have loved you, so you must love one another. By this everyone will know that you are my disciples, if you love one another" (John 13:34-35).

Did you get it? He says it *three times* in a row: Love. One. Another.

And that second sentence alone wraps up the whole relationship model: between God and human ("as I have loved you") as well as human and human ("you must love one another").

Jesus was cognizant that the world needed to see the truth about relationships, and we need to listen carefully. It's not a fault of humanness; it's the way God orchestrated the world to be.

WE NEED EACH OTHER

I hear pastors and teachers tell students all the time, "All you need is a relationship with God and your life will begin to fall into place."

So students begin a regimen to find God. They pray more, they attend youth group, they constantly try to be better at their faith practices, but then they find more emptiness—and more questions. They wonder, "Why would you leave me, God? I've done all You've asked me to do." But the bottom line is that He never intended for you to be alone. Nowhere in the Bible does anyone say you have to be a lone-ranger Christian.

I see students give their lives to God all the time. They believe that God is going to come in their lives and everything is going to be better. Some have been convinced that with a mere confession of faith, life will just immediately be a paradise here on earth. They fail to realize, however, that God neither makes life fall into place nor intends for anyone to walk through life alone.

This is where theology meets practicality.

Don't misunderstand: It's not *my* declaration; it's God's. He's the one who told Adam that loneliness is an unacceptable practice in the world *He* created.

But much of our time as believers is being funneled to a false sense of relationship. We believe we can have a relationship with God and God alone if only we read our Bible more, go to church enough, confess our sins, and practice the spiritual disciplines set out by the ancient church leaders.

Life isn't about who can make it as a lone ranger.

This life is about connectedness with one another.

It's about learning how to give.

It's about learning how to serve.

It's about learning how to find joy in the context of another's life.

When Buddy the Elf says, "I just don't belong . . . anywhere," it's because there is a lack of understanding of how people work around him. Buddy is searching for someone, anyone, to help him feel that "togetherness" we're all searching for. But as we watch, we see the unwillingness of everyone around him to recognize the need.

Buddy is different.

He's bigger than the elves.

He's jollier than the humans.

He's been given the gift of joy, and when he stands out in the normal society, he can't find union with others.

But at the end of the movie, when Buddy is understood by people around him, and as he begins to understand their world too, *Elf* stands out as one of the greatest Christmas movies of all time.

Why?

Because at one time or another, we all feel like Buddy.

We all feel as though we just don't belong.

We all feel as though no one understands where we're coming from.

We all want to have an inkling of understanding of someone else.

We're all looking for someone to connect with.

By beginning at the beginning, we can clearly see how the Creator of the universe set up successful living. He never intended for us to walk through life alone.

He gave us each other.

CHAPTER 2

THE ONLINE CONNECTION

THERE ARE FEW times in history when a revolution changes the way civilization sees and works in the world.

THE INVENTION OF FIRE

Can you imagine living in a world that didn't know how to start a fire? Think about all the things we do that require the simplest form of mechanical reactions.

We eat by fire.

We make things by fire.

We heat by fire.

We socialize by fire.

We travel by an engine that uses gasoline to produce fire.

If you took fire out of all the things we do as a culture, there might not be much to speak of. (And there would be a whole lot of cold people standing around.)

THE INVENTION OF THE WHEEL

Think about all the things we do with the invention of the round mechanical device we call a wheel.

We drive cars with wheels.

We fly planes with wheels.

The insides of machines have various uses for the wheel.

We have wheelbarrows to move stuff.

We have tractors with wheels to farm stuff.

We have bikes with wheels for transportation.

The invention of the wheel has dramatically shifted the way we do life here in the world, right?

Imagine a world without the wheel.

THE INDUSTRIAL REVOLUTION

The period of industrial revolution not only shaped how we work, the production value of a culture, and the definition of a family unit but also changed the way we live in the Western culture.

Cars are made in factories.

Phones are made in factories.

Clothes are made in factories.

Computers are made in factories.

Even food is sorted and packaged in factories.

Not much of our world would look anything like it does today without the Industrial Revolution. It's allowed us to produce more stuff, at a faster pace.

But one of the unintended consequences of the Industrial Revolution is the loneliness it produced. There was a time when families worked together and friends needed each other, but now we all go away to build companies away from our communities.

THE INVENTION OF THE INTERNET

I know this seems like a trivial section, but think about how many normal functions of today's life wouldn't be available without the invention of the Internet.

There was no such thing as Google in 2000.

There was no such thing as YouTube in 2002.

There was no such thing as Facebook in 2003.

There was no such thing as Twitter in 2004.

No iPhones.

No iPods.

No iPads.

No need for a laptop.

With the invention of the Internet, our culture has exploded with potential. We can buy things, sell things, play games, and connect on a different level than ever before.

The Internet has changed the way we do life.

It's changed the way we connect with others.

We don't send handwritten letters; we have e-mail.

It's given us a platform where we can have "friends" on Facebook. We can follow people on Twitter. We can even see people face-to-face using Skype.

It's a revolution that changed the way we do, well, everything.

THE ILLUSION OF CONNECTION

I'll never forget the summer of 2005.

Each year I hire about a hundred college students to come to Colorado to work with teenagers in the context of high mountain adventure. We call our camp KIVU, and we've seen tens of thousands of high school and college students find a place here they can call their home away from home.

This particular summer, I was downtown with one of my employees, and we were having coffee at a local coffee spot. We were talking about friendships, connecting people, and various adventures we both facilitated that summer. Then he brought me over to the bank of computers set on the far wall.

"Braner, you gotta check this out," he said.

He launched the browser on the computer and typed in www .facebook.com. Up came his picture and a litany of information he was using to declare his spot on the Web.

"See, you can connect with anyone who is connected on this thing. All my classmates, college friends, and teachers are on here. If you want to get a hold of someone, this is how to do it."

At that time, you could access Facebook only if you had a college e-mail address. I was already out of college, approaching the birth of my second child, so I just looked through my friend's profile.

I couldn't believe it.

I looked at my friend and murmured, "This is how we will connect in the future."

At the time, Facebook had only a few hundred thousand subscribers, but today it boasts of more than eight hundred million.[1] I couldn't believe the way you could use this simple website to connect with people of common interests. If you liked mountain biking, Facebook would populate all the people in your school that liked mountain biking and you could literally set up a trip with someone you might not know. If you liked making cupcakes, all you had to do was click on the hyperlink and Facebook automatically showed everyone in your area that liked making cupcakes. At the time, this was revolutionary.

With a click, you could update hundreds of friends of your current status. With a click, you could share an entire photo album with those same hundreds of friends. With a click, you could create a movement by setting up groups and networks. I was seeing a revolution equal to that of fire and the wheel.

I remember trying to explain Facebook to a group of youth leaders after my coffee session. I reserved a conference room and set up a projector, and when they all came in to hear the presentation, they laughed in my face.

"That will never take off."

"It's just another fad."

"How are we supposed to manage all those people in one spot?"

It was amazing, and I couldn't stop thinking about the potential.

Lo and behold, Facebook has become a mainstay of communication in our world today. People have Facebook as their opening page when they launch their own personal Internet browser, and studies are showing that we spend more time on Facebook than we do anything else in the world.

But one feature caused me a little concern. To connect people to your network, you had to become "friends."

IT'S MORE THAN A CLICK

I was concerned with the use of the word *friend* from the very beginning. It seemed as though we were transforming a word held with high esteem to something you could have with the click of a mouse.

So I started asking some of the students I work with . . .

What is the meaning of friendship if all I have to do is click a button?

Do you think we are watching some radical shift in the meaning of friendship?

I'd already seen a shift in cell-phone use as we started censoring our phone calls and preferring to text. What is this new "friendship" like on a wider network?

After watching Facebook garner the attention of the world, I've seen some incredible benefits, but I've also started watching some devastating consequences. The friendship Facebook offers is much like driving a car through a neighborhood. We have acquaintances who live in the neighborhood, and we have the chance to roll the window down on our imaginary vehicle, stick our heads out, and yell, "Hey, everybody!"

We can create messages much like e-mail.

We can post pictures of our lives, but we control what everyone sees.

We can fill our profiles with information, but rarely do I see someone post something embarrassing, confusing, depressing, or showing weakness.

It's an illusion.

Friendship can't be just about shouting out the window of a car.

It's more than showing the perfect photos.

Friendship has to be accompanied by experience.

Friendships are formed when we have a chance to celebrate someone else's accomplishments. Friends get to see the pure joy on our faces when we encourage them in their success.

Friendship happens when people know you care for them in a time of need. They sense the body language we posture as we put our arm around them and mourn with them through tragedy.

Friendship is being able to tell stories about how we climbed a mountain together, survived the class everyone else failed, or pulled a fast one on a teacher.

The *illusion* of friendship is making everyone in the world think we're perfect.

The world we live in today holds great potential for communication and connection, but what happens when we're communicating only an illusion of reality? When people are friends with just the person they see on Facebook? When people like you only for your homecoming-parade wave out the window of the car?

Don't get me wrong: This revolution is amazing. I've connected with people I haven't seen in years. People have the chance to see what I'm up to (at least what I want them to know), and I can see what everyone else is doing. It's unprecedented.

But I often wonder if the reason we feel so alone is because somewhere, instinctively, we know it's all a sham.

It's not true friendship when someone wishes me a happy birthday after they've been reminded on some toolbar. Remember when people actually took time to remember our birthdays?

Remember how valuable you felt when someone showed up at your door and asked you to come with them?

How about the time when everyone at school was getting together and they asked you to join them on an adventure they were planning? Didn't you feel special to be in the decision-making process right there, in person?

I know Facebook affords so many advantages, but with the convenience of networking comes the bad ideas of relationships along the way. Even though we have access to unlimited connection, there's something missing.

Instead of time spent experiencing life together, we've turned our world into a self-shaped, self-regulated, self-indulgent, me-centered life. We don't have a chance to be woken up in the middle of the night to help someone because we can just say, "I didn't get the message." If someone tries to invite us to a party, we can just use the now old throwback, "Ahh, I didn't see it. Did you post it on my wall?"

The reality of the situation is, with all of this technology involved, we're losing the ability to connect with each other at a human level. The networking capability is incredible, the connection to old friends and family is awesome, but the real-time relational building is becoming a thing of the past.

IT ALL STARTED WITH A TEXT

Texting was the first major shift.

About ten years ago, I was trying to set up a party for senior high students, and I started calling cell phones. The cell-phone craze was just taking off, and every one of my students had one.

I remember calling one of the students in my ministry, over and over, and I kept getting put off to voicemail.

I texted him.

He texted me right back.

I thought, "Okay, I know you weren't on the phone. Why didn't you just answer it?"

And then it hit me.

We are now a culture that wants to deal with relationships on our time.

We want people to fit into our schedules.

We need the distance to be able to push life to the side and focus on the things *we* want to focus on.

That's just not what relationships are all about.

Relationships are work.

They're inconvenient.

They're exciting and spontaneous.

You can't apply some formula for relationships and expect to walk out of the room with a load of friends.

Friends need attention.

Friends need help.

Friends need encouragement.

And so much of the time, we're not able to give the attention and encouragement they need because we're trying to make sure they fit into our worlds.

(Okay, I'll stop.)

Texting is a great technology, but it loses something. We can't hear the tone in someone's voice. We don't hear the inflection that tells us if a compliment is sarcastic or sincere. We miss that dramatic pause when we're about to hear something exciting. We reduce a cacophony of infectious laughter down to "LOL." We don't even have to spell correctly.

(I have a friend who teaches junior high who says the number of papers being turned in with text language—LOL, JK—is astonishing. Don't do that!)

PLUGGING IN = DISCONNECTION

So how does this leave us feeling all alone?

Maybe it's because something happens when we take human spontaneity out of the equation. When we can calculate someone's response, it takes out a bit of the human factor. I truly believe it has given us a false sense of belonging. And the irony? With all of these friends and followers and contacts and connections, I believe the biggest plague in the teenage nation today is not knowing who you can connect with.

We have thousands of friends on Facebook.

We know we can text our friends at all hours of the night.

We tweet to our hundreds of followers.

But in the end, there's no real satisfying or unifying connection because we've regulated relationships to technology.

UNPLUG AND RECONNECT

I'm not saying technology is bad. I just think we need a break from time to time.

We need to turn off the texting, power down the cell phones, fast from Facebook, and relearn what it means to be human again.

The most exciting times in my life have been spent with friends: when we rode our bikes over big mountains, rafted through white water together without falling out, and tried to conquer a business idea no one else thought was viable. Whether we succeed or fail, relationships get stronger, stories become legends, and connection is more than a tweet or a poke on Facebook.

You just can't do that over a cell phone, on your Facebook wall, or in a chat room.

If you have hundreds or even thousands of friends on all the social networking sites and still feel as though there is a dark hole of loneliness plaguing you, maybe you need to take a step back and ask honest questions about who the most important people are in your life.

Who can you go to when it all falls apart?

Who will join you on the platform when you win the race?

Who is going to stand with you when the world turns its back on you?

Will your Facebook friends be there?

If we took a look at the ways we try to connect with others, would there be some sort of consistent platform where we feel as though people let us down? Maybe the popularity of social networking isn't simply an easier way to connect but rather a way we can get around the potential rejection and fear that someone might not like us.

Or maybe we've just been taught the wrong ways to form friendships. Maybe we've been trained to give friends the attention of a click. Maybe we've been taught to share only our perfectly posed photos and cleverly coined statuses. Maybe we've been told that as long as we succeed, friends will follow.

But what if it's all been a lie?

CHAPTER 3

ONE BODY, DIFFERENT GIFTS

In Christ we, though many, form one body, and each member belongs to all the others. We have different gifts, according to the grace given to each of us.

— Romans 12:5-6

Be all that you can be.

— The Army

FOR WHATEVER REASON, millions of uncles all across the land feel the need to ask their nephews, "What do you want to be when you grow up?"

Okay, it's not just uncles. We all wonder from time to time, *What do I want to do?*

Fireman, doctor, policeman, pilot.

Remember dressing up like your favorite superhero? I can remember running into the tree house in our backyard, pretending it was on fire, and running out with people who were trapped in the back room.

I remember dressing up like a doctor at Christmastime using a Fisher Price plastic stethoscope to try to figure out all my uncle's heart issues.

Then in high school, *Top Gun* came along. I daydreamed about being a naval pilot, flying F16s through the sky at Mach 5. Now, that was the life! Even as teenagers, so many of us wore our aviator sunglasses to try to look the part.

Ah, yes, everyone loves a hero. But what happens when reality hits and you're not the hero you've always dreamed of being? What happens when you wake up and you're just normal? Or even worse—a complete failure?

I believe much of our loneliness is centered around the core fact that we can't perform to whatever level we think we should. We set expectations that we can do whatever we put our mind to, but the reality of life is that we are all created for different functions. As Paul said, "There are many members, but one body" (see Romans 12:4-5).

Western culture affords us the ability to think, *If I try hard enough, I can be anything I want.* The American dream is to find a profession that you wake up to every morning with a smile, give yourself away, make a lot of money, and retire a happy, fulfilled, elderly golf player.

LET'S GET REAL

But really?

Is that actually how it works?

Can you put your mind to *anything* and be *anything* you want to be?

Let's be honest here.

I have a friend who trains NFL athletes in the off-season.

He runs gyms that are full of the who's who in professional sports. So I had to ask.

"Tell me who comes into your gym. Do you ever see anyone famous?"

As I fished around for famous names, do you know what I found? *Nobody.*

I had no idea who he was talking about.

"Who is that?" I asked again and again.

He laughed.

"Are you telling me that none of the big-name quarterbacks are working out in the off-season?"

"Oh, it's not that. Here's how it works. Have you ever heard of the bell-curve theory?"

"Of course," I replied. "Most everything we know and test can be plotted on a bell curve with 20 percent low, 60 percent average, and 20 percent high. Right?"

"Exactly!" he affirmed. "That's exactly how professional sports work. Twenty percent of the athletes in the NFL are on the bubble, and they work and work, only to get cut from the team in the off-season.

"Sixty percent of the players will work hard, but let's be honest, the NFL needs hundreds of athletes to get the game going. So if you are big and of average speed and can make plays on the field, you're going to make it.

"Now, here's where it gets tricky. Even though 20 percent of the NFL will be at the top of the game, it's only 5 percent that most people could list by name. You know those players you can rattle off without thinking about it? Those guys have no need to jump in my off-season workouts. They're just gifted."

"Gifted?" I asked.

"Yep. They're gifted," he said.

Isn't that an interesting phenomenon? We've been told all our lives that we can be whatever we want to be, but in order to be an elite NFL athlete, you just have to have the gift.

I'm thirty-five years old, weigh two hundred pounds, and am slow as an ox, so I'm never going to play in the NFL, the NBA, or the MLB. It's just not going to happen. No matter how hard I work and how much I dedicate my life to a dream I might have, there's a calm reality that says statistically it's not going to happen.

Sorry to burst your bubble here, but that's true for most of us.

WHAT'S *YOUR* GIFT?

All of you who are working hard for a dream, I don't want you to be discouraged. But I do want you to think, *Am I really cut out to do this?*

I met another friend who is an executive of Major League Baseball. During one of our talks, I asked him, "How many people are actually going to make it in the big leagues?"

You want to guess what he said?

"Look, Andy, everybody knows there are those with a gift and those without."

Yep. Then he continued.

"There's about 20 percent of the players we draft who we know are going to play on television. Everybody else is just playing catch with the remaining 80 percent."

So what does that do to our dreams?

It crushes our drive to be the best we can be, right?

Actually, no.

In my day, every basketball player in high school thought there was a chance he could grow up to be just like Michael Jordan.

But guess what?

There is only one Michael Jordan. There will only ever be one Michael Jordan. His body was the perfect fit, his drive was the perfect mix of ambition and reality, and he was born to play basketball. It was evident from the moment he started puberty.

Did he work hard? Sure. That's what separates good players from great players, but there are millions of people in the world who could shoot five thousand shots a day and never make their high school basketball team.

It's just a natural function of our creation.

The reality of life is, God has gifted you with an enormous amount of talent to change the world, but only you can melt it into His desire and purpose for you. It requires a partnership with God, a perfecting of the gift He has placed inside of you. It's amazing to consider that you are a part of that plan. Think about it: God gave you a purpose, a reason, and even specific tools for you to partner *with Him* in this world to change it and His people in the ways He intended.

The problems arise, however, when your expectations take a different turn from the gifts you have been given. That's when failure, disappointment, and loneliness begin to creep in.

Imagine what it would be like to try out for a Major League team and find a group of people there who were gifted to be baseball players. They all throw longer, jump higher, swing harder, and run faster than you do. Sure, there might be a certain amount of work you can do to improve, but in reality, you find you just weren't born to be a baseball player.

I had a friend in college who was an Olympic icon. At the time, he ran the two hundred faster than any other human on earth. Each spring, he came back to the track at college and started working out to get ready for the spring trials. From year to year,

I would ask my friends if they could notice a difference in his speed.

"I think he's losing the speed, Braner. I even beat him by five seconds today," a friend bragged one year.

Then, about two weeks later, all the "average" guys had their tongues hanging out as the Olympian came into form and started running the way he was created to run. *Two weeks* was all it took for this guy to go from eating junk food and lying around playing video games to an Olympic athlete. It was unfathomable.

I think the sooner we discover what God made us to be, the sooner our lives can come into stride with our gifts and the sooner we can find joy and fulfillment. Without this tandem discovery, we are doomed to wonder what our gifts are and why life isn't working out the way we thought.

So how do we move from thinking we've failed at life to waking up every morning and knowing we are doing what we were made to do?

Look, I get it.

We all want to travel around on a tour bus, have fans throwing themselves at us while we make millions of dollars. It's a given. But in reality, God didn't create us all to be rock stars. Agreed?

I mean, how many times do we have to watch the *American Idol* first week of auditions and wonder, *Are you serious? Did you really think you were going to be the next big thing?* The last season, I heard my wife tell the poor girl on TV, "Honey, there's a reason they told you to run offstage and never look back."

You know you think the same things.

But seriously.

There comes a time in life where we have to recognize what we're good at and be realistic about the gifts we've been given.

It's no secret: I'll never play in the NBA.

I'll never play in the NFL.

I don't even know how to play hockey without hurting myself let alone all those poor souls skating around me.

I'm not fast enough for soccer.

I'm not smart enough to be an astronaut.

But the sooner we can eliminate the things we know we're not good at, the quicker we can begin piling up the areas we excel.

One of my all-time heroes is a man named Stephan Moore. Stephan is a seven-foot giant who played basketball for the University of Arkansas. Right from the beginning of this story, you have to understand that the University of Arkansas is a shrine to all things sports if you live in the state.

We don't have professional sports.

We don't have *anything* (that I can think of) uniting the state together beyond the sporting programs. The Hogs are *the* show in town, and you can count on it. Whenever the Razorbacks play basketball, the whole state shuts down until the game is over.

I remember watching Stephan Moore when I was growing up. He played for a coach named Eddie Sutton, and he was dominating the college basketball scene. He posted up most of the best players in college basketball at the time and scored like a champion.

One day Stephan came to our church to share his testimony and I waited in line for his autograph. As a twelve-year-old boy, Mr. Moore was my idol.

As fate might have it, we ended up working together when I graduated from college. Yep, that's right. I got a job right alongside my childhood hero. It was a dream come true!

We traveled the country together recruiting for a small summer sports camp, and I was in heaven. I asked him about playing for the Razorbacks and going up against some of the best

Division I athletes. Hearing all the stories from the locker room made me salivate with envy.

I'd get on a plane with Stephan and he had to bend over just to walk through the main cabin. Everyone was making comments about how tall he was, and Stephan just put everyone at ease saying things like, "Well, they sure don't make these things for guys like me, do they?"

Everybody just laughed.

They knew it.

They knew he was made for something different than the rest of us.

It was then I realized, Stephan was created to play basketball.

He didn't have an option.

Come on, what are you going to do when you stand seven feet tall and can jump out of the gym?

God gave him a talent, and he found it.

Luckily, America has a love of basketball, so it was an easy find. But some of us need a little extra help.

We have to take a real close look at how God made us.

What gifts did He equip us with?

How did He fashion us to function in this wide, wide world?

If we can take this seriously, we can begin working through another big cause of loneliness: the feeling that we are out in the world with nothing to offer.

So let's take a little inventory.

1. What do you like to do?
2. If you had the chance to do anything you wanted right now, what would it be?
3. Who do you look up to the most and why?

4. If you could make a million dollars doing whatever you wanted to do, what would it be?

Growing up I worked at a small Royal Ambassador camp in Arkansas. My youth director actually took me there and introduced me to all the executive guys. I remember being able to program the events, work on getting people their cabins, help run the refreshment stand — it was awesome.

But I also remember thinking, *There's no way I can ever make any money doing this.* It was only part of the summer fun. Everyone else had real jobs back home.

The retreat/vacation business is really hard to work unless you've got millions of bucks backing you already.

But I've been doing it for fifteen years now.

You know how? The Creator of the universe Himself is backing me. God fashioned me to do what I'm doing, and I love it!

The fact that I can sit here writing this book to you, to educate about God, to help you learn about relationships and work on a feeling of togetherness in a big world — it's an awesome thing. But I didn't go to school specifically for this. I actually graduated with a degree in theater and performing arts.

I love performing. I feel alive when I'm acting. I love the design of the set, the light configuration, the costume development, and the music choices to help an audience understand the story line. But the truth is, God has gifted me to talk with teenagers.

My peers think I'm crazy.

"Braner, when are you going to grow up and get a real job?"

And I often feel as though one of these days they're going to find me out. They're going to see that I'm doing what I really love to do. They're going to see that it's pretty easy.

But here's the secret: That's when you know you're in the right place!

MYTHS OF SUCCESS

#1: You can do anything . . . if you put your mind to it.

As an actor, I find it intriguing to watch the Oscar ceremonies.

Yes, I realize it's the height of narcissistic, celebratory gratification on the planet, but there's something about a gathering of one's peers telling the world, "Well done. This movie was worth watching." Often they get it wrong, and when I go to watch the movies nominated, I'm overwhelmed by the outright awfulness of movies today. But the fact remains: It is intriguing.

Every year, the Best Actor or Best Actress stands at the podium after receiving the ultimate award and says something like, "Dreams really do come true. If I can do it, you can do it. We all can achieve our dreams if only we put our minds to it."

Come on!

Do they really think people believe that?

Look, I'm not trying to be pessimistic here, and I believe dreams are good things to hold on to, but when kids start taking this stuff seriously, they really believe they can be *whatever* they want.

I believe another contributing factor to loneliness in today's world is not actualizing your dreams. Oh, sure, it's great to talk about the times your dreams came true, but what do we do when they don't?

One of my dearest friends has dreamt his whole life of being a software engineer. He's played with computers as long as he's known about them, and he's got the gift. He went off to get a degree in software development followed by a graduate MBA degree. He's consulted for small companies on their needs, and the guy has all the tools to make it work. But he can't find a steady job to save his life.

So is he in the wrong area of the country? Maybe.

Is God punishing him because he can't find a job that brings dream to reality?

No.

Does he need to work harder?

No.

He works harder than most people I know who make hundreds of thousands of dollars a year.

So what's the deal?

The fact that God has gifted my friend in so many other ways tends to sway my opinion. He's a great leader. He's a great people person. He lives to be outdoors. He wants to effect change in the lives of thousands on the planet. It's almost as if God has given him a dream but his gifts aren't matching up with the dream.

Imagine what it must be like to hear people you respect, people who believe in you, and people who invest time in your world saying, "Don't give up. Don't stop. Keep working and you can achieve anything."

Really?

I can achieve *anything*?

Sorry to say, there's no way on this planet I'm ever going to fly to the moon.

I'm not going to be an NBA center.

I'll never be an NFL quarterback.

I'm not ever going to main-stage at Madison Square Garden.

It's just not the way God made me.

And while many of my peers say, "Why do you have to be such a glass-half-empty kind of guy?" I find it incredibly freeing to know who I am. I love the fact that I know what *I can't do*, because it ultimately narrows the scope of what *I can.*

I know I'm a teacher.

I know I'm a compelling storyteller.

I know I've been given the ability to hold the attention of an audience to present information.

I know that. And functioning inside that gifting gives me ultimate joy.

When you realize what role you have to play here on the planet, the most beautiful sense of belonging begins to awaken inside your soul. The world begins making sense. No matter what you're doing, if God has gifted you in it, you're going to have a high level of functioning.

So, you see, I'm not saying, "Don't dream big." I'm not saying, "You *can't* do anything you put your mind to." But I guess what I am proposing is that you line up your dreams with your gifts, with the ways your dreams *can* come true.

Recently, I ran into a friend of mine who teaches junior high band. Junior high band? Can you imagine? Each and every day you go to work knowing you're going to hear some of the worst orchestral music of all time.

The trumpets are going to be flat.

The oboes are going to be sharp.

The percussionist is going to beat off-time.

"How in the world can you do that?" I asked him.

Being the smart guy that he is, he had the right answer: "I go to work every day knowing I'm going to shape the life of another human being. I get a chance to introduce Mozart, Beethoven, Debussy, and the great composers of our day. Is there anything better than that?"

I wanted to lean over and say, "Uh, yeah! There's a lot better than that." But I didn't. I just marveled at the pride my friend takes in his job. It's what God created him to do.

Paul talks about this concept in Romans 12:6-8:

> We have different gifts, according to the grace given to each of us. If your gift is prophesying, then prophesy in accordance with your faith; if it is serving, then serve; if it is teaching, then teach; if it is to encourage, then give encouragement; if it is giving, then give generously; if it is to lead, do it diligently; if it is to show mercy, do it cheerfully.

Can you imagine a world where we all knew what we were created to do? And then imagine what that might look like if we each had the opportunity to really function at a high level. Imagine serving one another in our own specific gifts.

What would it look like if a businessman, who is predisposed to understanding money, thought it was his job to serve the poor rather than lining the corporate coffers?

What would it look like if the farmer was more interested in feeding a population than making enough money to buy the latest farm equipment?

How might the world turn if everyone who had the gift of hospitality found a way to function inside their gift and serve all those around them?

Imagine that.

God gave each of us special gifts so we could give to each other and function as a whole body of people.

Now, that's revolution!

#2: You can do anything . . . if you study hard and get good grades.

Bill Gates is a Harvard dropout.

Steve Jobs didn't finish college.

Michael Dell had limited post–high school education.

Enough said.

#3: You can do anything . . . if you work hard enough.

When I was a freshman in college, I had four roommates.

And we had a blast!

I've never seen four guys want to work on the unity of friendship like those four guys did. It was such a great lesson for me to watch as they served one another.

I remember that one of the guys was set on being a physician. Back in the nineties, med schools were beefing up the entrance requirements because it was the best way to make a high-end living at the time. Of course that was before the HMOs, attorneys, and drug companies began taking over the health industry. But that's beside the point. One of my buddies was interested in becoming a physician, and I was there to support and love him through it.

He studied for at least eight hours every day.

He worked on the MCAT practice tests.

He worked at the hospital during the weeks.

He was a teaching assistant for the most influential biology professor at our university.

He did it all.

Four years of working . . . working . . . working.

He applied to several medical schools around the country and watched as letter after letter was delivered to the mailbox. "We regret to inform you . . ."

Every time he went to the mailbox, we held our breath in hopes that this was the one to let him in. And every time, there was another rejection.

Conventional wisdom says, "Just keep going; it will work out." So he did.

For the next *ten* years, he kept working, applying, studying, and applying, but every time he applied to another med school, he got rejected.

"Andy, what is the deal?" he asked one sunny Sunday afternoon.

"Brother, I'm not sure. This doesn't seem to be adding up." I mean, if anyone was supposed to have a chance at med school, this guy was the poster boy.

You know why it wasn't adding up?

He wasn't supposed to be a physician, and God had His hand on my friend's life. Sure it took ten years for my friend to figure it out, but he's now working at a university as a biology professor, and he couldn't imagine doing anything else with his life.

I believe in hard work—don't get me wrong.

If you have a gift, if you find joy in what you're doing and want to become a physician, it's going to take *a lot of work*! My friend is a doctor today, just not one that works in the hospital. He's now a part of a university biology program and has found a new love in teaching and helping students understand the issues in biology. But he never would have explored being a teacher if medical school had given him a shot at being a physician.

Isn't that awesome?

To know God has a plan for our lives.

To know He has the best plan for our work.

To know He created us special for something that may or may not even be on our radar right now.

What must it feel like every day to wake up and believe you're never going to be good enough?

What happens when you look in the mirror and ask yourself, *Why can't I look like someone else?*

What about the times you fail? If failure is simply a product of survival of the fittest, we're destined to wonder if we can ever amount to anything in this world.

But if there is a real God, in a real universe, who created us for a purpose, how can you be anything but overjoyed that there is a purpose for you?

It doesn't mean things are going to be easy.

It might mean we have to go through some hard times to discover what He's created us to be.

It might even mean we have to endure pain and suffering before we can actualize His will for us.

But to rest in the fact that there is a plan is reason enough for me to buy into the notion that there is a God and He loves us.

And that's just it.

FAITH IS NOT MAGICAL FAIRY DUST

For some reason, we've been convinced that to believe in God is some sort of mantra that everything is going to be okay in life. We're all going to be successful and popular if we just commit our lives to God. But let's not be too quick to buy into an idea that has no biblical basis whatsoever.

The greatest heroes of the Bible traveled long, difficult roads. They suffered greatly and were rejected by their peers. At one time or another, they abandoned it all—subjecting themselves to loneliness and despair—to follow the whispers of God.

Noah had to build an ark to the jeers of his peer group.

Moses was banished from the pharaoh's kingdom.

Abraham longed for the moment his son would be born, which didn't happen until he was late in life.

David was chased by the king for much of his life, and after he became king, he gave way to being an adulterer and a murderer.

Paul was persecuted on many different occasions.

And Jesus . . . Jesus was crucified.

So this idea that you can just commit to God and work to be successful in your faith flies in the face of the trans-biblical story, as all the characters of the Bible endured much in the way of change, sacrifice, and suffering.

The ultimate story of redemption is held in the hope we have that all things will be made right again. But in the interim, we are all people who need to walk together with others to find purpose.

Sure, we need a relationship with our Creator.

Yes, we need to spend time working on our faith.

But we also need to know that in spite of all our work of self, there is an intrinsic need to have others walk alongside us through the joys and hardships of life. No matter how strong we become in our faith, we will always need each other.

And that's where encouragement comes into focus.

THE VALUE OF ENCOURAGEMENT

The best gift you can offer someone is encouragement. The four words "I believe in you" can literally change a life.

In 2004, I was at a speakers' workshop in Colorado Springs. Yes, those of us who spend our lives on the road communicating to people often attend meetings to hone the art of communication. After all, according to Dr. Paul L. Witt of Texas Christian University, "The idea of making a presentation in public is the number-one fear reported by people in the United States."[1]

The workshop gave each of the attendees topics different from their regular topics and shot video of each member speaking on his topic. It was super helpful to watch a film of myself as I started looking at how an audience might perceive the message according to my own body language. I remember the facilitator being pretty critical of one of my presentations, and I walked out of the room feeling like a huge failure.

You know how it is, right?

You try really hard to achieve a goal and impress your peers only to find out you weren't as good as you thought. It's humbling, to say the least.

After the presentation, I was walking through the hallways when I ran into a guy named Wes. He saw that I was down, depressed, and in need of a little encouragement, so he walked up to me and chose to engage.

"Tell me a little about yourself, Mr. Braner," he started as he peered down at my name tag.

And that's where it began.

Since 2004, Wes has been a crucial part of my life. He introduced me to what it meant for someone to come alongside another and encourage. He's not patronizing; he's honest. But in every conversation, he says, "I'm with you and for you."

Wes began walking me through a systematic approach to life. He coaches me through the core of who I am and shows how the rest of my life needs to be in response to that. For example, when we went through our first session, the purpose of my life became clear: "Love God. And love others." My core is based on Matthew 22, when Jesus says, "'Love the Lord your God with all your heart and with all your soul and with all your mind.' This is the first and greatest commandment. And the second is like it: 'Love your neighbor as yourself'" (verses 37-39).

With the concept of loving God and loving others at the core of my existence, I go through exercises to make sure that my financial life lines up with the core. Wes examines my professional life, my recreational life, my marriage life, my father life, and much more. His ability to speak into my everyday life is invaluable.

I can't tell you what it means to have someone whom I admire look me in the eyes and say, "I believe in you."

But a word of caution: Encouragement can also work in the other direction.

I recently talked to a baseball player trying to make it to the big leagues. His dream since he was in Little League was to play professional baseball.

He played in college.

He was drafted.

He went to training camp, and the team cut him.

His life started spinning out of control because everyone always reinforced his significance surrounding baseball. He found purpose when he stepped on the baseball field, and those watching could identify him as someone special.

Now that baseball is gone, he's reeling.

How many of us have similar stories?

Someone told us we were good at something, so the dream of achievement crept in to mingle with our purpose and significance. When the dream didn't come to fruition, what were we left to do?

When we have people in our lives who reinforce our significance in an eternal way, saying such things as "I believe in you," it makes all the difference in the world. If only my friend had a mentor in his life who took the focus of significance off baseball and started giving him purpose in how he lives life, I wonder where he'd be today.

I'm grateful to have someone in my life who assures my significance on a regular basis and ties nothing to it. "I believe in you" carries more weight in my life than the next speaking gig or book

I write. "I believe in you" means I matter to someone in the world.

Take a second.

Put this book down.

Think about who is in your life that needs to hear "I believe in you" to repair the damage of significance created by culture.

Now go tell them they matter!

Do you remember who the Super Bowl champions of 2003 were?

What about the NBA champs of 2003?

The top five Billboard songs of 2003?

Okay, what about your second-grade teacher? Soccer coach? Youth leader?

When I ask audiences these same questions, guess which ones they can answer.

That's right. The last ones.

Not the multimillion-dollar sports celebrities. Not even their favorite songs. But they remember those people who influenced or spoke into their lives.

Isn't it amazing?

How much time, energy, resources, and emotion do we put into the buckets of life that really don't make a difference to us *at all*?

The concept of having some*one* in life to pull us out of normal day-to-day routines and give us the encouragement we need to make it often overshadows the some*thing* we'll achieve if only we "work hard enough."

Don't get me wrong: Hard work and dedication are important factors as we help people understand significance, but in the end, our short lives are shaped by the relationships we make along our own journey. And if those relationships are filled with people who believe in us, the lonely factor fades away and we are recognized for the abilities we do have rather than the ones we don't.

Paul said it clearly: "I remind you to fan into flame the gift of God, which is in you through the laying on of my hands" (2 Timothy 1:6).

What can *you* do to fan someone else's flame?

Who in your life fans *yours*?

ALL FOR ONE

The biblical approach to significance and belonging is clear. We are the body, and God is the head of that body. He has lavished on each of us a special gift, a vital function that we must do in order for the whole of the body to work correctly.

First Corinthians 12:4-6 says it like this: "There are different kinds of gifts, but the same Spirit distributes them. There are different kinds of service, but the same Lord. There are different kinds of working, but in all of them and in everyone it is the same God at work."

Some have the gift of leadership, while others of us have the gift of creativity.

For some, giving is a gift.

For others, encouragement is a gift.

And still others have the gift of compassion and relationship.

The gifts that exist in the whole of humanity are as colorful as a kaleidoscope making brilliant colors of life. Why would we want to change someone's color to match our own agenda?

Consistent with the biblical point, without the ear, where would the sense of hearing be?

Without the eye, where would the sense of seeing be?

You see, every part is necessary for every other part to be successful.

We need eyes to see what the ear is hearing.

We need ears to alert us when we hear something going on around us.

All the parts are important.

What would it look like if, instead of everyone trying to be an eye, we were comfortable with the gifts God gave us?

Everyone wants to be a celebrity of some sort. As a society, we sense more value in singers, artists, and athletes. So if we want to fit in, we have to conform our own gifts to match those receiving the most attention.

But what if I'm not an athlete? Does that mean I'm not valuable to society?

You see where this is going?

If we create environments where these gifts can be developed and celebrated in their entirety, we will begin to meet that need to feel significant, filling that little gap in our hearts, that little part of us that wonders, *Do I matter in this world?*

CHAPTER 4

WALKING IN THE DARKNESS

WHY WOULD YOU, as a teenager, ever suffer from depression?

Come on!

Let's be honest!

You don't have to deal with a mortgage, a car payment, deadlines for your job, or any of the pressures adults deal with, *right*?

WRONG!

Walking in the dark halls of depression may be more common than you think. About 20 percent of teens will experience depression before they reach adulthood.[1] Twenty percent. That means if you're in the car with four of your friends, one of you will likely experience depression in your teenage years.

So what makes this lonely feeling of depression take over in the teenage years?

Let's look at three types of depression and see why you and your friends may be particularly vulnerable.

RELATIONAL DEPRESSION

Teenagers are social people.

Even the most seemingly introverted teenager is looking for some kind of community to connect with. It starts in elementary school on the playground, but when puberty sets in, there's a whole new set of issues.

Hormones are firing on all cylinders.

A sense of value and worth becomes central to a teenager's self-awareness.

Teenagers begin modeling what they see in relationships around them, whether at home or in the media.

And everybody wants to have friends.

Have you ever felt as though you wanted to be with someone but they just wanted something material in return? Or have you ever felt like others have hidden agendas?

"What do they want from me?"

"Why are they always asking me for something?"

"Why do I feel like I have to act excited every time I'm with them?"

That's the basis of relational expectations. One person sees a friendship or a relationship one way, while the other has a totally different set of requirements. To be honest with you, this is the first sign of the rising tide of depression that can wave over us.

When our life is filled with friendships we are unable to quantify, conflict starts confusing our natural brain functions. We were created to be in union with one another from the beginning of time. When the intent of togetherness comes into conflict by unrealized expectations, we find ourselves in dark places.

When expectations aren't met and two people find out some kind of secret hidden from their obvious intent, they're left with a void. It's like a black hole devouring any sense of worth, right from our souls.

We thought they were our friends.

But they were only out for themselves.

We thought they were on our side.

But they betrayed us.

Darkness sets in.

You can't get out of bed.

You can't go to school.

You can't get your mind off it because the darkness is consuming.

Then the questions start . . .

Is something wrong with me?

What did I do?

Why didn't they value me?

And the answers are worse . . .

No one likes me.

No one cares if I live or die.

There's no chance I'll ever connect with someone.

You can tell you've entered the darkness when you can't stop thinking about how much you *don't* matter. The world begins to spin, and all your thoughts hover between insignificance and worthlessness.

You start thinking . . .

I'm a failure.

I'll never amount to anything.

I can't go anywhere.

This is the black hole of depression.

I was working with a student once who had recently ended a relationship. He thought they were made to get married; she thought otherwise. He thought they were doing great; she was already looking around for someone else. He confided in a friend; she started liking his friend. They broke up, and she began dating the friend.

Depression!

Some might say, "Just get over it. People break up every day." But depression isn't something you just "get over." There's so much more involved biologically, spiritually, and relationally.

A lot of people have no idea what depression looks like or the various ways depression can creep into our lives. It's a real feeling, a true emotion, and the more isolated our culture becomes from one another, the more we'll hear of depression washing over certain demographics.

Loneliness is one of the by-product feelings of depression, and I think it's important we talk about it here.

BIOLOGICAL DEPRESSION

In 2001, my second daughter was about to be born. We were so excited to have the chance to increase our family with a new daughter; there was pure joy in the air. My wife was eight and a half months pregnant, and we were painting the baby room and getting everything in order for our new baby to arrive. We could hardly wait.

I remember walking outside my office one day, and my wife was walking along the sidewalk. Hobbling was more like it. A really pregnant woman has a tough time just moving around.

I could see the panic in her eyes, and I knew it was time.

We whisked off to the car, got the luggage we'd already packed, and drove a hundred miles per hour to the hospital. The thrill of knowing that my daughter was coming in the world coupled with the fact that my wife was beginning to experience real pain was almost more than I could stand; the adrenaline pulsing through my veins was almost palpable.

When we got to the hospital in Colorado, the doctors escorted us to the room, and four hours later, Maggie was here.

I remember holding Maggie with all kinds of pride. She was my first daughter, and as I looked into her little eyes, I knew life was different. It's one of those times in life dads of daughters just know.

A few weeks after we were released from the hospital, I recognized something different about my wife. She was edgy. She wasn't her normal upbeat self. She was worrying about a lot of things that she didn't normally worry about.

It's one thing to have a bad day, or even a bad week, but this was going on longer than what someone might consider a bad time in life. Something wasn't right.

We had a doctor friend from Phoenix staying with us at our teen facility in Durango, and he came to me. "Andy, I think your wife might be suffering from postpartum depression."

"What? What is that?" I'd never heard of such a thing.

He was telling me how some women go through a depression time as the hormones in the female body start recalibrating after childbirth. From time to time, I would hear about a mother strangling her kids or leaving her kids in a strange way, and my doctor friend helped me see how someone could think like that.

"Mothers aren't designed to be sociopathic. They love their children. They want the best for their children, but sometimes they need a little medical help to get through the hormonal transition."

We took it seriously.

I talked with Jamie about the new information I learned, and she willingly agreed to be tested by a professional. Our new doctor prescribed some medication and helped us see all sorts of depression symptoms.

Depression isn't just something you can casually throw to the sidelines. It's a real thing. People suffering from depression have thoughts of loneliness and hopelessness and sometimes don't want to get out of bed in the morning.

Some of my faith friends tried to counsel us during Jamie's depression. They would say things like, "You guys just pray, and the Holy Spirit will take that depression away" or "Give it up and give it to God." Of course they meant well, and I believe in the power of spiritual healing, but sometimes biological depression requires medical attention.

Postpartum depression isn't the only depressive situation. I counsel teenagers frequently who have given up on life. They find their grades at school failing. They don't have invigorated passion for much of anything. They walk around the house in a lethargic state, and often I hear, "I just don't care anymore."

Sure, there are times when we all have to go through a trying situation to learn how to hear God speak a message of hope to our souls, but sometimes it's okay to seek help from a medical professional. Depression isn't something to mess around with. Statistics show that depression can be a starting point for all kinds of other issues.

For instance, 30 percent of teens with depression also develop a substance abuse problem. They're also more likely to have less success at school, in relationships, and with their careers. They're more likely to engage in promiscuous activity, putting themselves at risk for pregnancy and disease. They catch physical illnesses more easily. And perhaps most seriously, the number one cause of suicide is untreated depression.[2]

SPIRITUAL DEPRESSION

In order to understand all facets of depression, however, we must consider what the Bible tells us: "Our struggle is not against flesh and blood, but against the rulers, against the authorities, against the powers of this dark world and against the spiritual forces of evil in the heavenly realms" (Ephesians 6:12).

We can't just look at our circumstances on the outside and make definitive claims as to what's wrong. Sometimes the feeling of loneliness can be a spiritual issue.

When Jamie and I first moved to Colorado, we started a new business, bought a new house, and adopted our second boy from Africa. All seemed well on the outside.

But deep down, something wasn't right.

The world decided to go broke.

Family issues started creeping in.

The adoption process was harder than we'd anticipated.

We were trying to develop community, find a church, and make new friends.

It wasn't long before all of those things collided and I started feeling inadequate. My prayer life went something like this: "God, You called me to this deal. I didn't call You. You put the spirit of adoption in my heart, and I'm almost certain You asked us to move across the country. As we look for a church, get in the community, and try to work on our marriage, God, I just need some help." I felt as though something was terribly wrong.

I felt like Moses probably felt when he moved the entire nation of Israel from Egypt to the wilderness. Remember that story?

The story is found in Exodus 14.

Moses had just freed the people from the grips of Pharaoh where they'd been slaves. Pharaoh used the Israelite nation to make bricks for all the buildings the nation of Egypt wanted to build.

Every day, bricks.

Every day, sweat.

Every day, they had to meet the quota of bricks or the Egyptians made their lives miserable.

When Moses came to bring a message of freedom, the Egyptians weren't really excited about the proposition. Remember God's plagues? The Nile turned to blood, the locusts swarmed, the frogs came in, and in the end the firstborn sons of all Egyptian families were killed.

Finally, Pharaoh broke down and decided to let the Israelites out of the bonds of slavery.

They were on their way. They knew that God had promised them a life full of success and freedom. For the first time in generations, families were going to be free. They were singing and dancing on their way to the Promised Land.

And then Pharaoh changed his mind.

In Exodus 14, the story begins with the nation of Israel wandering through the wilderness. They came up on the Red Sea, and when they turned around, they could see Pharaoh's army coming after them.

Can you imagine?

Hundreds of thousands of Israelites standing in the middle of the desert were witnessing the greatest military force the world had ever known, chasing them. They were no match for what was coming. They knew that if they stood on the banks of the Red Sea, Pharaoh's army would ride in and slaughter every man, woman, and child.

They knew that if they took the plunge into the sea, many would drown.

They knew the livestock would die.

They knew the elderly wouldn't have help.

And they knew the children who didn't know how to swim were sure to be lost forever.

They knew there was no hope.

And they started questioning God's promise in their life.

What happened to a land flowing with milk and honey?

What happened to freedom?

What happened to all the promises God made to the nation?

The Israelite leaders approached Moses and said,

> Was it because there were no graves in Egypt that you brought us to the desert to die? What have you done to us by bringing us out of Egypt? Didn't we say to you in Egypt, "Leave us alone; let us serve the Egyptians"? It would have been better for us to serve the Egyptians than to die in the desert! (Exodus 14:11-12)

Can you imagine the hopelessness that comes over someone when they think of the hope God promises as they see the reality of disaster at the forefront?

Not many of us will face the Red Sea like the nation of Israel.

Not many of us have to beg for slavery over the prospect of being slaughtered.

But in the middle of a depressive time, it feels the same.

And those feelings are *real*!

The person suffering from spiritual depression sees the world between the prospects of drowning in the Red Sea or getting slaughtered by the armies to come.

I knew God called us to adopt.

I knew He wanted us to continue ministering to teenagers.

I thought I was doing exactly what the Lord wanted us to do.

I was walking in the freedom God promised, but my outside circumstances didn't seem to match up with those promises.

I struggled every morning to get out of bed.

I didn't feel we had a real purpose.

I couldn't see God moving in the way I thought He'd promised me.

I was in a spiritual dark place.

There were times I thought to myself, *Just take me back to Egypt! At least there I knew what I was doing.*

And here's where hope meets darkness.

It didn't happen immediately.

It wasn't some epiphanous moment.

But something happened in my soul that took all the worries away.

In Exodus it happened at the very last minute.

Right before Pharaoh was to run the nation through with his military might, God provided a way out.

He gave the Israelites a dry crossing right through the throngs of the ocean.

Can you believe that?

In my state of spiritual darkness, right before I was ready to hang it all up, God rescued me. He gave me a peace, unmistakable. You've heard the saying "the peace that passes all understanding"? Well, that's exactly what happened to me.

After months of individual prayer, weeks of friends praying for me, my circumstances didn't change, but my soul found rest.

The only way to overcome spiritual depression is to continue to seek God's supernatural waves of peace.

He alone is the rescuer of my soul.

He alone knows where I'm struggling.

He alone put His loving arms around me, and in the end I felt a calm whisper say, "It's all going to be okay."

I'm not one to prescribe the "give it up and give it to God" cliché, but something happens when you stop focusing on your circumstances and give credence to the fact that God has the whole world in His hands.

After all, if we really believe that God created the world . . .

If we really believe He sent Jesus to rescue us from our sins . . .

If we really believe that His providence throughout history drives mankind closer to a relationship with Himself . . .

How can we fail to recognize that He cares for each one of us in our time of need?

The Bible says, "Before I formed you in the womb I knew you, before you were born I set you apart" (Jeremiah 1:5).

David sang out,

> You created my inmost being;
>   you knit me together in my mother's womb.
> I praise you because I am fearfully and wonderfully made;
>   your works are wonderful,
>   I know that full well.
> My frame was not hidden from you
>   when I was made in the secret place,
>   when I was woven together in the depths of the earth.
> Your eyes saw my unformed body;
>   all the days ordained for me were written in your book
>   before one of them came to be.
> How precious to me are your thoughts, God!
>   How vast is the sum of them!
> Were I to count them,
>   they would outnumber the grains of sand —
>   when I awake, I am still with you. (Psalm 139:13-18)

And it was Jesus who said, “Surely I am with you always, to the very end of the age” (Matthew 28:20).

If God has promised the hope of a relationship with Him, then no matter what circumstances come my way, I can find hope in Him.

And the gospel is all about hope.

Every religion on the planet tries to answer the issue of hope. Questions of afterlife, hope for a better now, living a better life, and the myriad of promises offered from any faith are all designed to architect a view of hope.

Teenagers ask me *all the time*, “Andy, why do you follow Jesus?”

And to be truthful, I can begin to explain what I think are simple theological reasons.

I can talk through Creation.

I can work through apologetics to prove the Bible to be true.

I can tell them the joy I have in my life.

But at the end of the day, the only reason the gospel makes any sense to me is the fact that it ensures hope through God’s involvement here on earth with mankind.

There is a hope that someday all the evil will fade away.

There is a hope that someday I will stand with my Creator.

There is a hope that disease will be cured, death will no longer be a part of life, and the ills we see happening all over the world will right themselves in a way to give testimony to God’s providence.

Without that hope, I’d stay in bed too.

CHAPTER 5

NOBODY CARES

AT THE END of 2011, a young man came home from school with a burden weighing on his soul. The kids at school were making fun of him for his feminine tendencies. They called him names like "fag," "queer," and "queen."

The young man was troubled enough to end up writing a letter to his sister and parents, and in the end he took a rope and hung himself.

Can you imagine?

Can you actualize people taunting you enough to push you to take your own life?

Well, that's exactly what's going on in the hallways of today's high schools.

Sure, there are some of you who fit into a particular crowd and find your niche, and others who have a home life equipping them to survive the latest self-image disaster. But what happens when we feel that absolutely no one cares? I mean *really* cares.

Sure, your mom is supposed to say you look good, you're smart enough, you're good enough. But who is really out there believing in you? Who, apart from those who are *supposed* to love you, really says you're worth something?

With a lack of positive feedback, it becomes really easy for us to listen to all of the negative messages out there. In particular, there are four lies we believe that lead us to a spiraling state of loneliness.

LIE #1: I'M THE ONLY ONE FEELING THIS.

This one is straight out of the playbook of Eden. Remember when God created Adam and Eve in the garden? (see Genesis 1:26). Remember when He told them they could eat of any tree they wanted except the Tree of the Knowledge of Good and Evil? Remember when the serpent approached Eve and said, "God knows that when you eat from it your eyes will be opened, and you will be like God, knowing good and evil" (3:5)?

I can almost hear Eve's thoughts: *You mean I'm the only one who doesn't know what God knows?!* It's classic.

Fast-forward to modern times . . .

We believe there are people out in the world who have life all figured out.

We've convinced ourselves that if we have the right clothes, drive a nice car, and live in a big house, all life's problems will go away. We'll have what everybody else has.

But it's not true!

Hollywood makes art that looks cool.

The music industry is all about presenting an image.

Athletes walk around trying to convince everyone they're not *just* playing a game.

And when we're on Facebook, we see only the best in people. Nobody is posting pictures of the depressing times.

Nobody is submitting the weaknesses of personality on their profile.

Nobody is being *real.*

We're hiding our relationships behind the screens of our computers for the sake of control. Control *we* have to muster in order to create the illusion of rightness is exactly why social networking is so popular.

We want to live like we want to live, so we've created an alternative universe where everybody seems to have the same ideals as we do. But behind the computer screen, we still wonder, *Am I the only one who feels alone?*

After she climbs into bed, *This fashion really doesn't make me feel any more together.*

After the big game, *Is this all there is?*

Kids are watching friends have parties, not struggling through issues. Hip-hop artists only post the good pictures to bolster their brands. College students are trying to impress future employers. And all for the sake of being the someone we *want* to be, not being who we *really* are.

So let's set this straight: You are not the only one who feels alone! *Everyone* on Facebook is asking the same question.

Every athlete is asking if he or she really matters to anyone.

Every celebrity deals with insecurity.

Every musician wonders when the ride will end.

Every student wonders, *Do I really matter?*

If the sum total of your significance comes in the form of comments on your Facebook wall, you fall right into this category.

If you are looking to Twitter to provide you with enough friends to make a difference, you're living here.

If you find yourself in the dark of your own room, feeling all alone, welcome. We're all in this together.

LIE #2: NO ONE WOULD MISS ME IF I DIDN'T SHOW UP TOMORROW.

One night after I graduated from high school, the phone rang late in the night. My friend was on the other end of the line, saying, "Braner, Chris just found out his brother shot himself in the chest."

There's *no* book to prepare you for this one.

There's *no* podcast to help you navigate.

There's *no* way . . . anyone . . . ever . . . is supposed to endure a loved one's committing suicide.

It's just not natural.

To have to bury a child is the worst nightmare a parent could ever dream.

And this was one of those times.

I was close to this family. We went to school together. We played basketball together. We basically grew up as extended family, and now to find out the older brother decided to take his own life?

How does this sort of thing happen?

The American Adolescent Child Psychiatric Association claims suicide as the third leading cause of death for people aged fifteen to twenty-four years old.[1] There are several factors that contribute to the whys of suicide.

Depression.

Substance abuse.

A family history of abuse.

Psychological disorders.

Previous suicide attempts.

A feeling of loneliness.

Loneliness causes people to think that taking their own lives is a rational solution. They feel as if there is no one in the world who cares for them, so what difference does it make?

In fact, the loneliness can take over every part of our identities, and it gets to be so warped, the thoughts start to surface: *I'll show them. They might not care about me now, but I'm about to make them care*. And the ideas of suicide come full circle.

Why do we live in a world where people even have to wonder if anyone cares?

Have you ever heard of a teen suicide where no one cares when a student dies?

Have you ever been to a funeral for a teen when no one showed up?

Have you ever been to a funeral where it turned into a party because someone died too early?

See what I mean?

How do we allow ourselves to feel so lonely that the only cognitive solution to our needs is to take life?

Because we don't think about it.

We're not perceptive enough to see when someone is really in trouble.

The act of suicide can't be relegated to the person who chose to take his own life. If we all belong to this world, we all hold a level of responsibility when someone in the tribe is feeling a sense of worthlessness.

As a culture, we've got to start asking ourselves honest questions, starting with *Why?*

I wrote of depression in an earlier chapter, but the reality of depression is something we can address.

Substance abuse can own a person, and I wrote of addictions and what it means to be an addict.

But there is no reason we should be allowed to feel all alone.

Can you imagine what a mother feels like when she reads a note from her son saying, "No one cared about me."

How many phone calls would she have made to prevent her son from killing himself?

How many friends would have stopped the busyness of life and make time for him?

How many siblings would have let him know he meant something to them?

Then why don't we do that now?

I'm so tired of hearing about teenagers who think the only way out is to end their lives. It makes my heart sad because I start wondering what I could have done.

Let me put your mind at ease right now: There are plenty of people in your world who care about whether you wake up in the morning. Life is too complex to think in the simple terms of "no one cares."

We all have someone out there who knows our name and wants to know what we're doing. Living in a technologically connected world has provided a relational matrix image that we all need, but sometimes the hurt of loneliness comes with unrealistic expectations. We watch a celebrity use Twitter to announce important events to their followers and see automatic responses. So when we don't feel the same attention paid to our account, there is an unrealistic expectation. I saw this in the summer of 2010.

Conan O'Brien was going through a mess at NBC. I don't know if we'll ever know what actually happened, but Conan was fired and started a comedy tour across the country. He used Twitter to announce that the tickets were on sale for the upcoming tour, and I followed the ticket sales as they sold out of every show in a week. One week!

Unfortunately, that same reaction and attention isn't available to just anyone who signs up for Twitter. But the expectation is the same. Teenagers wonder why when they post something, only a small number of viewers pay attention.

There are a few different issues colliding around this concept:

1. Your generation is growing up in an online world, and that world is keeping score. This generation sees the numbers of viewers, followers, and friends quantified everywhere they look. They know how many people are out there.
2. This same generation has a misconception of personal value. Nobody wants to start work in the mail room and work to the CEO position. This generation is starting to perceive that they are entitled to the CEO position when they graduate from college. Nobody takes into account Conan's years spent on the comedy tour, the late-night show he hosted, or the fact that he headlined national news with the NBC debacle. It just doesn't register.
3. So unrealized expectations are met with the idea that no one cares. It's a mysterious problem but a real one, nonetheless. All too often when our unrealistic expectations are met with realistic results, we don't understand why, so we attribute it to those three words.

Which leads me to the third lie creeping into the minds of the lonely . . .

LIE #3: NOBODY UNDERSTANDS ME.

I must admit freely, I get this.

It's not unusual to live in a world where most feel that nobody "gets" them. Just to be honest, this feeling of misunderstanding is a natural cycle of events in a normal family dynamic. When we're young, we need the attention and provision only parents can offer.

I've seen this in my own family. Three years ago, we adopted a young son who was dropped off at a marketplace when he was three. That's right, three years old and this little guy was left to fend for himself. He spent a number of days wandering through the marketplace begging for food, working for attention, and just trying to survive.

When the nuns of a Catholic orphanage saw my son day after day, they knew he didn't have anyone looking out for him, and they took him to the local orphan facility. The transition from the orphanage to a permanent home has been a tough one on my son and my family. We have provided him with a roof, food, and education most American kids enjoy from the time of birth, but there's always something in the back of his mind that wonders, *When will this all stop?*

He eats fast.

He clamors for attention.

And he tries to make sure we're still going to be there when he needs us.

It's natural for a young child to express the needs only a parent can give. When children go through adolescence, it's the first time in their existence they can begin surviving on their own.

As teenagers, you can fend for yourselves, to a certain degree.

If you're hungry, you open the refrigerator.

If you're thirsty, you grab a water bottle.

If you want to play, you can find your shoes and go outside to play with your friends.

There is a natural cycle of transition a child goes through from needing the attention and provision of parents to being able to live independently. But it's in this transition that you may still wonder, *Who's looking out for me?*

You might strive for affirmation from peers.

You may look for the nod of approval from teachers.

You seek places where you can have foundations of security.

These needs are real.

The feelings that drive us to wonder if anyone likes us are completely natural. But when we try to go out and live life on our own, we set ourselves up for failure.

We need each other.

We need approval from the people around us.

We want to know confidently that we hold a place of purpose in the lives of people we care about.

So what happens when life gets busy? When all those people need the same confirmation but no one takes the time to reach out and say, "I approve of you"?

Teenagers begin the long spiral into depression.

No, let me take that back. *We all* begin the long spiral into depression.

I have a friend who used to play football in the NFL. From the days of Little League football, people have approved his performance on the field. In high school, he was the talk of the town. He admits that in college, he barely had to tie his own shoes because everyone thought he was superhuman.

But there came a day when he couldn't run as fast.

He couldn't hit as hard.

He didn't make the big-time plays that once came effortlessly.

So he retired.

Throughout his whole life, people identified him as a football player, and now he was stuck at home wondering where he fit in the world. This is a common thread among second-tier professional athletes. They've made enough money to fuel their ego, but when the money dries up and the fans aren't screaming their names anymore, life suddenly produces doubt: "Does anyone really care about me?"

I've spent countless hours talking with my friend about the value he adds to his community. I've tried to help him see that football was only a season, but now life has so much more to offer him. Still, the celebrity image he was living has been reduced to a place where the rest of us live.

Loneliness.

Step back and think about the culture we are growing into. Everywhere we turn, someone is being recognized for something, but it's all smoke and mirrors. Celebrities are celebrities only for the fact that they are celebrities. They don't produce anything; they just appear on the cover of tabloid media. It communicates to us, "If you want to mean something, you have to be in a magazine . . . or have a thousand Facebook friends . . . or five thousand Twitter followers." If you don't match up, no one cares.

What a lie!

The solution is a cultural anomaly. We've got to get back to developing meaningful relationships with people outside of the online antics we're playing today. It really doesn't matter how many people view our pictures on Facebook. The only way we can help curb the feelings of aloneness is to live life together.

Back in 2005, I made a conscious effort to help our staff here at KIVU see the difference that living life together can make. At KIVU, we stepped down off the stage and shifted our staff focus from coaching kids *through* life to actually experiencing *with* them. We got all kinds of comments from teens about the difference.

"I can be myself here."

"At school I find myself in a box my friends create, but here I can be honest."

"Thanks for letting me be me."

The result was a whole new theme for the camp: "We live life *with* kids, not *at* kids." And it has revolutionized the way we develop real-world relationships.

When we can submit our own feelings of worth from "Hey, look at me!" to "Let's live this life together," things change. Feelings of loneliness begin to fade away, and the dark shadows of purposeless existence don't matter. It takes only one person to encourage us to watch those old lonely feelings fade in the distance. We only have to take a look around at the community developing in our immediate surroundings and see that we are valuable people.

LIE #4: I HAVE TO FACE THIS ALL ALONE.

The cold winter feeling of being alone can be overwhelming. The frigid longing for someone, anyone, to reach out and know who you are and what you're going through can be a desperate feeling.

I know.

I'll never forget playing basketball in high school. It was one of the greatest times of my life. I can remember the cheers from the fans, the acceptance that I belonged to something bigger than myself, and the way it felt to belong to something.

But I have to be honest. Even though I was on the basketball team, and many of my friends would say I had nothing to feel lonely about, I never really knew who was with me. You know what I mean?

I never knew who was on *my* team or how they were going to

respond in a difficult situation when life came between me and them. It was hard to navigate.

My freshman year was especially hard. My best friend and I both tried out for the varsity basketball team, and my best friend was really good. He was so much more talented than I was, but we'd been playing together for a long time, and most everyone knew us as a duo.

We ran wind sprints to get ready for the tryouts.

We ran the offense we learned in eighth grade.

We played against some of the high school guys to prove we could hang with them.

But in the end, when I went to read the list of guys who were on the team, my name wasn't there.

The coach decided he was going to take the opportunity to make sure we had identities of our own. He didn't think it was a good idea for the both of us to continue being on the team at an equal level, so I would start for the JV team and then be an extra guy for varsity, while my best buddy started for varsity.

I know it's a tough world.

I know there are times when we have to learn how to win and how to lose.

But I felt all alone.

I didn't know if my friend really felt loyal to me. After all, he was going to be just fine starting for the varsity team as a freshman. I wanted to be happy for him.

I wanted to tell the world how proud I was to know this outstanding player, but my heart was crushed. And it led me to a dangerous place, a place alone.

So many times, we isolate ourselves from the rest of reality and think we are all alone. I wonder if it's the Enemy's most effective way to make us vulnerable and take us out.

You've seen the Discovery Channel, right?

Remember watching the pride of lions as they hunt the unsuspecting gazelles? The female lions go on the prowl, and they track down food for the pride. When they find a group of gazelles for lunch, they crouch in the grass to walk as slowly and quietly as they can so as not to be seen by the wary animals. The Discovery Channel producers cue the deadly music as the lions pounce from their grassy hiding place, and you can watch the pride split the herd.

Lions know the effectiveness of isolation. It's no wonder the Bible says that the Enemy "prowls around like a roaring lion looking for someone to devour" (1 Peter 5:8). If the Enemy can isolate you from the group and make you feel all alone, you are vulnerable to be *lunch*!

It's the same way that Satan approached Jesus in the beginning of His ministry. He waited until Jesus was alone in the desert to pounce. The Evil One knows how to destroy.

REJOICING WITH THOSE WHO REJOICE

Paul got it.

He understood the difficulty in developing relationships. He traveled all over the known world trying to connect people with the message of the gospel. In one part of Paul's writings, he says, "Rejoice with those who rejoice" (Romans 12:15).

Rejoice isn't a word we use in our daily lexicon. In fact, I think I'd be hard-pressed to remember the last time someone used it in daily conversation. It's a word commonly reserved for holidays, birthdays, and special occasions. Rarely do we find the need for such a word in the twenty-first century.

Still, for believers, it's our responsibility to understand how

Paul meant to use the word in the context of our lives today.

I think I have an illustration.

Can you remember the last time a friend got a new car?

He rolls up in his driveway, and instead of pulling it into the garage to keep it nice and clean, he leaves it in the middle of the driveway for all to see. Sound familiar?

It might have seemed a little disingenuous, but at the heart of the act, the guy with the new car was trying to fill the void in his own life. He was looking for some sort of encouragement or approval through owning a new car.

Now, here's where you come in.

You see the new car in the driveway and you have a couple of response options:

1. The Covet Response. You walk up to the car as your friend is waxing it, and you say in a bit of sarcasm, "Hey, Steve, great car you got there." And in your mind, you're trying to find all the issues wrong with that particular model.

Or . . .

2. The Rejoice Response. You walk up to the car and in a genuine voice, you say, truly excited, "Steve, that is so awesome you got a new car! It's exactly what you needed, and I think this is the greatest car out there for you. Could you take me for a ride?"

Now, who do *you* want to be friends with?

Exactly. Number two.

That's what Paul was trying to tell us.

We want to be friends with people who truly share our excitement for life. They rejoice when we rejoice; they're happy when we're happy. In other words, we love to be around people who are willing to share life's celebrations with us.

It builds the bonds of trust.

You find rest with people who are encouraging.

This is the way life is supposed to work. Rejoice. Together.

MOURNING WITH THOSE WHO MOURN

Likewise, Paul asked those in communion with him to mourn. He called on the congregations to recognize the times when their communities were going through hard times, to feel the pain together.

Let's have another illustration.

Imagine going to a funeral of someone who you cared for deeply. It might be a grandfather, a grandmother, maybe even a mother or father. This person wasn't just another ordinary human; they were a part of who you are. They contributed a significant portion of life to making you, well, *you*.

As you stand over the casket in the funeral home, knowing full well that we all die, someone walks up to you and says, "Well, we know he's in a better place."

What are you most likely to do?

Punch the person in the face?

Kick him in the groin?

You know you've heard it. You may have even said it. And you're not the only one. But instead of trying to make the situation better by saying the most trite clichés, might I make a suggestion?

STOP!!!

The next time you have a chance to walk through the journey of tragedy with someone, let that person know you're just going to be there for them.

You're not going to ask them to be theological.

You're not going to ask them to make any sense of "why."

You're not even going to out-spiritualize them with comments on heaven and the afterlife.

Nope.

You're just going to sit there with that person.

And cry.

Mourn with those who mourn. Find sadness in the pit of your existence that is just sad for the purpose of being sad.

I spoke at a pastors' conference on this once. The question on the table was "Do you think Jesus was really sad when He found out about Lazarus?"

The brilliant PhDs were certain Jesus couldn't be sad because He knew in a short time He was going to restore Lazarus to the land of the living. This, therefore, canceled out any sort of loss.

When it was my turn to stand up and be counted, I said, "Why couldn't Jesus just be sad for His friends? He saw that Mary and Martha were sad, and I think He just found it in Himself to express to the world that even God gets sad sometimes when death takes over."

Sure, God knows the end of the story when Life overcomes death. But have you ever thought about the idea that maybe God gets sad too?

Maybe when He looked over Jerusalem, it wasn't sadness for His own rejection; maybe Jesus was just sad for the people.

Sad that they were going to continue living under the reign of religious bondage.

Sad they were missing out on life and life more abundantly.

Sad they were content living in a world created for them but submitting to sin, which always leads to death (see Romans 6:23).

Why can't God be sad?

When we see God living life *with* us rather than *at* us, it is the difference in every other religion on the planet. We are given a model of faith in which God literally mourns with us in our saddest times.

What would it look like if we mirrored God's sadness in our own lives? Not to patronize others in their weakness but to feel the sadness they experience as if it were our own?

The bonds of trust built through celebration and mourning help us connect to each other in the confines of our own isolation and live together in a world built for us, together. We need to make sure we don't pay attention to the lies of loneliness. Don't let them take root in your life. And if they have, pull them up by the roots. The genesis of new communities lies in the foundations we create as we encourage, rejoice, and learn to mourn with every person in our world.

In doing so, we ensure that we are never really alone.

CHAPTER 6

CORE FEARS

WHEN I WAS in fourth grade, my father was called to a different job. We were living in Illinois at the time, and he entertained the idea of becoming a manager at an airfield in Little Rock, Arkansas.

When my parents sat us down and gave us the option of moving, I couldn't believe what I was hearing. We were going to move from the northern part of America down to some backwoods state known for the country bumpkins? Arkansas? Really?

I remember asking, "Are we going to have to learn how to chew and spit in class?" Halfway trying to get my parents to rethink their decision to uproot the family, I would use any line I could get a hold of to change their minds. There's something about people who live in the North; we think we're more civilized than the rest of the world. I know how awful that idea is. I've met so many southern friends who are wonderful, but the perception was my reality at the time.

Three months later we moved.

I was frustrated about moving away from my family and friends to somewhere I'd never heard anything good about, but

I figured it was a learning experience. So at a young age, I decided to go and explore.

For our first stop in Little Rock, my mother took us to the mall. I'll never forget walking up to the entrance. Lined up outside was a group of retirees waiting for a bus to take them down the road to watch the Arkansas Razorbacks.

They all had on red and white clothes.

They were carrying their Arkansas flags.

And a few of them even sported the hog hat and these small hog noses tied around their heads. It was a bunch of old people dressing up like farm animals.

I looked at my mother. "Are you serious?"

Then, as we walked up to the mall entrance and opened the door, I heard the most awful noise of my childhood.

"*WOOOOOOOOOOOO, PIG SOOOOOIE*," this group of retirees all yelled together.

This group of northerners just looked back and stared in amazement. It was the craziest thing I had ever seen. And I remember thinking, *Those people are NUTS!*

Three years later, I was putting on my own red jacket to attend my first college football game. I became a loyal Arkansas Razorback fan. I never played football officially. I never had the chance to be in the huddle with guys trying to score a touchdown. I never saw the snarl of an opposing lineman whose main interest in life was to take me out. I was just heading off to the field to watch the Razorbacks.

Soon I learned that the cheering I had heard in front of the mall that day is known as "calling the hogs." It's a staple of all true hog fans in order to call the hogs together before the beginning of the big game. And it didn't take long living in this community before I began to drink the Kool-Aid.

One thing you have to understand about Arkansas is there are only a few athletic teams to rally behind. There aren't any professional teams. There aren't any Major League Baseball teams, NFL teams, or even NHL teams to give the state a national identity. The Razorbacks are it! And I was ready to join them.

It's kind of a crazy phenomenon.

While I was growing up, every Saturday during football season, I saw the entire state shut down when the Razorbacks took the field. Businesses closed down. Grocery stores became ghost towns. Even the movie theaters had to adjust their showings according to the university football schedule. Traffic stopped in the major roadways because everyone in Arkansas roots for the Hogs.

I guess that's why it was such a major event for me to head out for my first game. All my friends kept talking about this lore of the Razorbacks. I remember walking into the stadium and seeing the green grass. I remember smelling the popcorn. I remember hearing the sounds of the band playing the fight song.

And sure enough, when it was time for the kickoff, I stood together with fifty thousand of my closest friends to call those Hogs to victory.

What I wasn't ready for was the popularity of college football sweeping the nation as ESPN began reporting in a twenty-four-hour news cycle. It doesn't matter if you're from Louisiana, Alabama, Florida, South Carolina, or Tennessee — Southeastern Conference football games are all pretty similar.

Everyone dresses up in the colors of their favorite team. The parking lots are littered with people partying before the game. Everyone attending the game knows the fight song and whatever official yell they'll need to root their team to victory.

Now, almost fifteen years after my first game, I'm still in a world of wonderment.

Why do we do this?

Why do we act like children to come together for a football game?

Why do some people literally hate someone because he or she wears the wrong color?

I read a story not long ago of an Alabama fan who decided to poison the trees at Auburn after the War Eagles beat the Tide for a national championship contention.

What is *that*?

Yet I wonder if the illustration of football fans can give us insight into the feeling of loneliness.

What makes a football game so exciting?

Is it the game, or is it the people we can experience the game with?

I can't imagine anyone actually moving to Arkansas and just starting to call the Hogs on his own. Nor can I imagine my going back to my old town up north and yelling, "WOOOO! PIG SOOOOIE!" Maybe once. But after that, I'd probably learn my lesson.

It takes a tribe of people to welcome others into the fold. There was a tribe waiting for my family at the mall that day. And while I quickly passed judgment on that strange, strange tribe, I soon found myself truly connecting with that community.

SIX COMMON ROADBLOCKS

In my own relationships, as well as through talking with young adults across the country, I've found some common fears invading the ability to connect with others. These fears usually act as roadblocks, keeping us from experiencing a true connection with others.

1. Fear of Rejection

What if they don't like me?

What if they think I'm not cool?

If I wear this, they'll see how silly I really am.

I've got to have a new phone; all my friends have it.

Ever had these same concerns in your day-to-day life? It's interesting how we need to sense acceptance from those we admire. It drives us to do things we wouldn't normally do. We need to measure up and make sure they can't find fault in who we are.

I remember talking with David, a teenager who came to hang out with us for a while in Colorado. On the morning our program was going to start, his mother put him on a plane and informed him that he was going to Colorado to spend fourteen days in the mountains with teenagers from all over the world. Needless to say, David wasn't very happy.

Not only did David already have other plans with his friends for the following weeks, he had no idea who these people were whom he was about to spend two weeks getting to know. His core fear of rejection started playing in his head.

What if they don't like me?

What if I don't fit in?

What if they make fun of me?

They've never done the stuff I've done.

It took about two days before I noticed David's withdrawal from the others. I kept seeing him standing in the corner by himself, with an apathetic attitude, wandering the campus alone.

I decided to ask him.

"Hey, David! What's up?" I called across the field one day.

He walked the other way.

I walked a little faster to catch up.

"Hey, man, what's going on?" I asked again.

For the next hour, David and I talked about everything going on at home.

His dad was an alcoholic.

His mother was interested in her own social calendar.

He didn't make the lacrosse team this year.

His grades were plummeting.

He started smoking weed with his friends.

He didn't know if he could name any close friends.

David was walking through life all alone.

As we talked, I tried to reassure him that we were there to help him, love him, and serve him over a two-week time he would never forget. But David kept on, "But people really don't like me that much."

Instead of pointing out the obvious—that he hadn't given anyone a chance to like him—I told him about my own fears.

"Rejection is a tough barrier to get over, isn't it?" I asked. It's my core fear. I knew exactly what David was trying to protect because I do the same things.

I put up walls around my real self.

I try to show the world I'm an okay person.

I find validation in success, not in my own failures.

I often think, *If they only knew ____________, they wouldn't want me around.*

And David felt the same way.

There's no doubt that the feeling of rejection is one of the main culprits in relationships today. We feel unsure about people, and we tend to put up walls to protect ourselves from the first moment we meet someone.

What if they don't like me?

What if they make fun of me?

What if they don't want me around?

What if I don't measure up?

What if I'm the last one picked?

What if they find someone better?

Rejection can rule our lives. It paralyzes our sense of belonging and draws us into an introspective way of living. We calculate our every move based on what others find acceptable.

The fear of rejection is the first roadblock to connecting with others.

2. Fear of Judgment

A few years ago, I was at a school function and ran into a girl dressed in black.

Black fingernails.

Black hair.

Black pants.

Black shoes.

Black eyeliner.

The only part of her that wasn't black was her skin. She chose to wake up every day and put white makeup all over her face to make sure her face juxtaposed her clothes. It was kind of strange.

My friends started calling people who dressed that way "goth," and the rage for looking like vampires grew throughout the country. I don't know if it was Harry Potter or Twilight that caused it, but the fascination with the underworld was in full force.

The girl came up to me after one of my assemblies and asked if God could love her.

I pondered a minute, and her whole life flashed before my eyes. I saw a girl who struggled with fitting in. She wasn't taken seriously on the home front. I envisioned a girl who grew up in an athletic world, but didn't have the skills to play soccer at the Y or kickball on the playground. Her siblings were probably successful, while she struggled to make sense of life.

"I know that God loves you just the way you are," I whispered. And I watched as a little tear fell from the corner of her left eye. For the first time in her life, she heard that God's love for her wasn't conditioned on what clothes she wore or how far she could throw a softball.

Judgment is just another roadblock often thrown up for us to deal with. We are uncomfortable when someone else takes a moral high road and exclaims the right way to live. Some fall into line and, coupled with the fear of rejection, tend to look like everyone else around them.

But for others, it's a challenge to prove them wrong.

I know how this works. It was a cornerstone in my own faith development.

I remember going to a Christian university full of Bible-believing, born-again Christians. Everyone had a background of at least going to church, if not being a youth-group leader while growing up.

I remember the first Sunday morning I slept in and missed my weekly church attendance. I didn't miss many Sunday services, so this was quite abnormal for a guy who grew up in a Christian home, attended a Christian high school, and then went off to a Christian university.

I walked down the hallway of my dorm and saw an open door on my way to the restroom. I peeked in to see a friend of mine putting on a three-piece suit. But he had slept in just like I had.

As I kept walking, I realized that the fear of judgment from those who actually woke up on time caused him to dress up like a churchgoer that morning.

It was the beginning of the end for me. I decided right then and there I didn't want to have anything to do with God, Christians, or anything "church." I knew there were people who were partying on Saturday night and waking up on Sunday pretending to be Christians, and I didn't want anything to do with it.

So instead of lining up and fearing rejection or judgment, I ran the exact opposite way. I decided I wanted to show them the level of hypocrisy they were tending to the world, and I was determined to make them come and tell me about it.

Judgment is a driving force in our lives. We either conform to avoid it or challenge the natural surroundings to force people into the corner of judgment so we can point out their weaknesses.

Sadly, the fear of being judged by someone has driven much of the church's work with teenagers to be a little mushy. We're afraid to tell our friends when they are in the wrong because the only thing worse than living in sin today is telling someone else they are.

3. Fear of Abandonment

I'll never forget the moment my wife and I decided to adopt. We ended up deciding to rescue two orphan kids from Rwanda. I'll never forget the feeling we had when we thought we were providing a salvation of sorts to two little Africans. But I had no idea what I was really getting into.

You see, for whatever reason, the strength of being a savior outweighs the feelings others might have when they're being saved. We thought we were doing this great work for the orphans, but what I learned is they were doing a great work completing our family.

Can you imagine what it would feel like to live in the abyss of abandonment?

Every day, my children wake up to five white people, and their skin looks totally different. It's a wonderful picture from the outside, but imagine what it must be like on the inside.

One afternoon, my little Gabby was sitting on my lap and I was telling her how beautiful her skin was. I told her how I wished I had skin like hers, and she looked up at me with those big brown eyes and said, "I wish I had white skin like you."

Now, I don't know if it was a reaction to what I was saying to her or if Gabby truly understood what she was saying. I don't know if she was trying to say, "I wish I looked like you," or if she was trying to say in her own way, "I wish I knew my real mom and dad."

Can you imagine the feeling of abandonment orphans feel when they think about their parents who left them? After all, God set up the family to be a place of acceptance and adoration, not rejection. But you know the beauty of God's design. He takes one person's loneliness and creates an opportunity for fulfillment and acceptance.

Romans 8:17 says, "If we are children, then we are heirs — heirs of God and co-heirs with Christ, if indeed we share in his sufferings in order that we may also share in his glory." God designed the universe in such a way that those who choose to follow Him are automatically adored rather than abandoned. God chose to allow for a way we can know Him as a father knows a son, or a mother knows a daughter. And so much more! If He knew me before I was "created . . . in my mother's womb" (Psalm 139:13), He knows me even more intimately than my earthly parents do.

There are few places in life that are supposed to be filled with acceptance, and family is certainly one of them. When we feel as though our family isn't a safe place, the fear of abandonment can throw us into loneliness.

4. Fear of Feeling Ignored

When our adopted son came home, I learned a lot about being ignored. Tiki was excited to be involved in everything going on in the family. He was always clamoring for more attention, good or bad.

He would smile for attention.

He would play for attention.

He would jump up and down on the couch as long as someone paid attention to him. We had to work really hard to learn how to speak Tiki's language of attention.

One of the hardest roadblocks to overcome is the fear of being ignored. When we need someone, anyone, to reach out and give us attention, often we resort to any attention we can get. Deep down inside of us, we want to be recognized. We want people to know who we are, and we want to know others. It's how God created us.

The Bible puts it like this:

> Formerly, when you did not know God, you were enslaved to those that by nature are not gods. But now that you have come to know God, or rather to be known by God, how can you turn back again to the weak and worthless elementary principles of the world, whose slaves you want to be once more? You observe days and months and seasons and years! I am afraid I may have labored over you in vain. (Galatians 4:8-11, ESV)

Scripture speaks of our need to "be known," but it also warns against our doing anything to turn back to the weakness of our own spirit. We were made to know and be known by God. And if this is true, if we were truly made to know and be known by the Creator of the universe, how much more should we fight to know each other? It is essential to overcoming this feeling of emptiness. We can't ignore and weren't meant to be ignored. The loneliness of isolation will always cause us to spiral into the deep dark shadows of depression. We must find a place of knowing.

5. Fear of Humiliation

There's hardly anywhere in the world where humiliation is a good thing.

I remember watching the ever popular *Jackass* movie series. For those who are unfamiliar, Johnny Knoxville decided to make a string of short Three Stooges–like comedy sketches and put them all together to form one long feature film.

The skits were incredibly crass and irreverent, garnering the series an "R" rating, but the phenomenon swept across the country. It's almost as if anything funny had to have something to do with the Knoxville gang.

Not long after the release of the films, I was watching an interview with one of the stars of the series. His countenance was different than in the movies. He didn't look like he was ready to be shot out of the cannon anymore. He didn't want to be known for a movie where all they did was humiliate each other. In fact, the crazy part of the interview was the obvious need for this actor to be taken seriously for his acting abilities.

This isn't surprising. We weren't made to just go out and be humiliated. It's a form of flattery when people laugh, but when the laughing stops, you often have to ask yourself, *Who really cares?*

That same type of feeling was the demise of one of the greatest comedy actors of all time, Chris Farley. Farley was the darling of *Saturday Night Live*, bringing us skits such as the Samurai, El Niño, and the family motivational speaker Matt Foley (who lives in a van down by the river).

Farley lived the high life. He partied with all the celebrities, ran with the who's who in Hollywood, and had a promising career. On December 18, 1997, he was found dead on the floor of his apartment in Chicago, apparently from a drug overdose.[1]

I can't help but wonder if the humiliation of being Farley's *Saturday Night Live* characters drove him to a vicious need for acceptance. He wanted to be taken seriously as a comedian and an actor, but in the end, maybe he couldn't find enough satisfaction to tame the need.

I used to watch VH1's *Where Are They Now?* and *Behind the Music* to find out what happened to the bands of the seventies and eighties. The common theme in all the stories was the need to be seen. They all just wanted to "make it," whatever that means. And most all of them wound up trying to find satisfaction in the drug culture or the wild world of sexuality.

What drives someone to continue to climb over the roadblock of humiliation to a place where the whole world finally looks up and says, "You've made it"?

6. Fear of Feeling Worthless

The final roadblock, or core fear, we run from in the lonely circle is the feeling of worthlessness. We've watched so many movies and television shows that drive us to make our lives matter. In fact, the Millennial generation is characterized by students who graduate from college needing to make sure their lives make a difference.

I took my son to watch the third Transformers movie, *Dark of the Moon*. I found it incredibly interesting to watch Shia LaBeouf's character, Sam Witwicky, try to get a job for the first half of the film. He was marching from office to office looking for an interview with someone, *anyone*, who would hire him.

He was offered a job in the mail room at a couple of different firms but kept turning them down because he had "saved the world from the Decepticons" and surely his life was worth more than a mail-room job.

It's exactly the need we all feel. We want our lives to matter. We want our time here on earth to count for something.

Worthlessness leads us to feel completely invalidated. We seek and search for meaning, and if we can't fill the void, we start the spiral.

"I'll never amount to anything."

"Life is such a waste."

"All I do is go to school, go to work, and come home."

"What difference does it make if I live or die?"

THE STORY OF THE BIBLE

I know it might be odd to headline the story of the Bible here, but let's just cut to the chase: The Bible addresses these core fears through a personal relationship with God.

Abraham looked for acceptance through his having a son. God provided.

Isaac looked for acceptance through the lineage of God's promise. God provided.

Jacob was a kaleidoscope of needy core fears. God blessed him after his wrestling with the angels.

Samson needed acceptance through Delilah. God ended up providing through his defeat of the Philistines.

Every one of the twelve disciples was in need of someone to make sure he meant something in his own right. Jesus provided.

Paul was looking for acceptance through the persecution of Christians. Jesus met him on the Damascus Road.

Every major character in the Bible was trying to deal with the core fears of humanity, and God ends up providing their every need in the end.

The beauty of God's story isn't heaven after death. No, that's just the beginning. The beauty of the story of God is His continued provision for our loneliness and fear of failure. In the end, the God of the Bible chose to meet us here on earth through the incarnation of Jesus Christ. It's the only difference between Christianity and *all* the religions around the world.

So if the core fears of failure, humiliation, and not being accepted are moving over you like a storm brewing, just remember God's promise: "Be strong and courageous. Do not be afraid or terrified because of them, for the LORD your God goes with you; he will never leave you nor forsake you" (Deuteronomy 31:6).

CHAPTER 7

ADDICTIONS

I RECENTLY FINISHED a string of autobiographies about pop and hip-hop acts. I read about The Beatles, Elvis, Madonna, Ray Charles, Jay-Z, and most notably Steven Tyler (the lead singer of Aerosmith) as he detailed his journey from snot-nosed kid to judge on America's top-rated talent show, *American Idol.*[1]

I guess I was interested to see if the larger-than-life people we see in the movies, listen to on our iPods, and see advertised in shopping malls all over the world were able to identify their core issues concerning success and failure.

Tyler's book is filled with foul language and questionable stories from being on the road as part of one of history's bigger-than-life rock-and-roll bands. But one thing stuck out: His addiction to sex and drugs ruled his existence.

He tells a story of having to hire gatekeepers to keep the girls at bay. He articulates the *need* to snort a line of coke just to make it through recording sessions.

The pain he describes as he tried to go to rehab several different times made me ask myself, *Is there anything I'm so addicted to that I would flush my life down the drain?*

We all know how dangerous addictions can be, right? I mean, all we have to do is tune into the latest VH1 *Where Are They Now?* show to watch the demise of almost every pop star ever in existence.

Can you think of one who made it?

The disco acts of the seventies all retreated into a whirlpool of drug addiction.

The hair bands of the eighties were addicted to the party. High sexuality, high substance, high all the time was the name of the game.

The grunge bands of the nineties were addicted to depression. They hung on to the pain of knowing the world wasn't going to spin their direction.

And in 2000 we introduced an era of watching young innocence swept away with the likes of Britney Spears, Christina Aguilera, Lindsay Lohan, and Miley Cyrus.

Addictions are dangerous, and they come in many forms.

Addiction to fame.

Addiction to substance.

Addiction to sexuality.

You can count on addiction to always lead us to the worst parts of humanity. And you can be sure that addiction isn't reserved for the rich and famous.

We have a teenage laboratory happening at KIVU in Durango, Colorado. It's an outdoor adventure paradise for kids ages thirteen through eighteen. We introduce teenagers to white-water rafting, fly-fishing, mountain biking, and a whole host of other outdoor adventures.

While the kids are having fun in the outdoors, we provide life-on-life training in the development of a Christian worldview. The teens get to ask intimate questions often taboo in their own spheres of influence back at home; nothing is off-limits.

Who is God?

Who is man?

Is God real?

Is the Bible really true, or is it just a book of fairy tales?

They have the chance to ask anything, anytime, anywhere, and I train our staff to listen well and answer with integrity. If they don't know the answer to a specific question, it's okay for them to say, "I don't know."

Over ten years, we developed a place for teenagers to explore the deepest issues they have to deal with. With the risk so low, the teens who come to KIVU are able to deal with some pretty intimate life issues, including a host of sexual addictions, specifically pornography.

Out of every ten guys I counsel, seven of them are addicted to online pornography. The online addiction to pornography is destroying the foundations of sexual awareness. Guys (and girls) are running to a false premise of what sexuality is really all about, and it begins to isolate them as human beings. They forget who they are, and they try to make up for their sin in different ways.

THREE WAYS PORNOGRAPHY AFFECTS TEENS

1. Reputation Protection

As a young man enters the multibillion-dollar porn industry on his personal computer, he has no idea what demons he's inviting into his life.

All of us have a large reputation that extends out over many social boundaries. We all know people, and we all put people in metaphorical boxes as we try to understand our surroundings.

Let's take Jeff, for example. I don't know Jeff that well. We don't spend a whole lot of time together. We certainly haven't shared any intimate details with one another, but I do see Jeff from time to time, and we laugh together.

I have friends who know Jeff too.

So every now and again, we get together, and I have a pretty good idea who Jeff is and how Jeff is going to respond in certain situations. I've put Jeff into a "good guy" box. He makes good grades. He's nice to his teachers and parents. He goes to church pretty regularly. Yeah, he's what we'd call a good guy.

I don't have any conflict with Jeff until he decides to react a different way than I expect. He jumps "out of the box," and then my brain has to figure out what to do with him. Why did he act that way? I would never have guessed that.

We all do this.

And everyone who we ever meet does it too.

So when a young man gives in to the temptation of online pornography, he has to protect the greater reputation he has with other people. He has to make sure he stays in his box.

So what happens if my friend Jeff decides to watch porn?

Well, we know that God is not in the business of tempting. James says, "When tempted, no one should say, 'God is tempting me.' For God cannot be tempted by evil, nor does he tempt anyone" (James 1:13). So, obviously, falling for these temptations isn't something a good guy does.

So what does Jeff do?

He's got to create a different reality. He's got to make sure he doesn't risk changing the box for the people who think he's a good guy. So Jeff is on the move.

He's secretly creating another box, another world where the life he's living can't be seen by anyone. This box is smaller and darker, but it keeps drawing him inside. And as long as he keeps up the appearance of the good-guy box, no one will even know this little box exists.

You know the circus man who spins fifty plates all at the same time? Jeff now has two plates. If he lets one drop, he's going to reveal his inadequacy to everyone watching. But the crazy part about it is that Jeff thinks he can manage spinning the plates.

Jeff starts thinking things like *I can handle this*, *I'm not hurting anyone*, *No one will ever find out*, and *I can make this work*. His addiction begins to grow in the shadows.

Now the real crazy part of this example is that most people think that Jeff is the coolest guy around. They don't see any problems. Jeff doesn't allow his reputation to be called into question for anything. Jeff is good!

It's one thing for Jeff to keep a broad reputation intact. After all, he doesn't see people all that often, and when he does, he knows they don't want to dig too deep into his personal life. He's safe. He'll be okay. Or at least he thinks so.

2. Protection from Those Closest to Us

Keeping up a reputation is easy to do with those who see us only in passing. But what happens when those who are closest to us start sniffing around our private lives?

These people are those who know us from the inside out. We've spent intimate time with them. This is a mother, father, sibling, best friend, or some kind of mentor or coach.

Jeff is now in a dilemma. His mom is starting to dig around, and she's going to find that other box, that smaller secretive box Jeff has been trying so hard to keep hidden.

Jeff is quickly becoming obsessed by his little secret box. He is now in defense-and-distraction mode, padlocking his box (his heart, his thoughts) to make sure no one can look inside. He's got the smoke and mirrors going to keep those closest to him confused and focused on *anything but* what he's really doing.

More and more often, he withdraws to his room and away from family outings. The history on his online account is erased every day. He watches porn only when he's sure no one is around. He is constantly preoccupied with making sure the tracks are covered.

He isolates himself from anyone having any reason to think Jeff is hiding something, and this is where the addiction begins to take hold of his heart.

He starts seeing women as objects rather than as people.

He starts thinking relationships are only something worth conquering, not nurturing.

He begins to dabble in online chat rooms and expands the circle of sin as he continues to remind himself, *It's okay; I got this. Nobody will ever know, and nobody will ever get hurt. After all, it's just me and my computer, right?*

3. The Final Stage: Extreme Isolation

Unless Jeff has found a community of porn advocates, he's now in a dangerous state of aloneness.

Jeff continues to live the life he started before his deadly addiction. He's still the same Jeff in the same box that people thought he was in at the beginning. The good-guy Jeff has fended off any inquiry from a broad reputation standpoint. He's done a good job keeping the demons at bay and has gained a lot of confidence in sneaking around because he hasn't been caught. And secret Jeff is doing a great job making sure no one close to him has any idea there is a whiff of a problem. This enables even more confidence and reassures Jeff he is a pretty good sin manager.

But now comes the ultimate test: Can Jeff find anything in

his life to remind him of the real world? Is there anywhere he can find honest integrity of life?

When Jeff tries to go to sleep at night, he closes the door to his bedroom and turns off the lights . . .

There's no one around except Jeff and God, and Jeff begins to wonder, *Who am I?*

You see, Jeff actually created three different personalities, and they can all be tied back to sin. Good-guy Jeff has no idea who secret Jeff is. Secret Jeff is trying to cover good-guy Jeff, and that only creates confused Jeff. The reality of who he is and who he needs to be has driven him to ultimate confusion. He doesn't know who he is anymore. He doesn't know how to reclaim himself. He has nowhere to go to find help; he's closed off everyone closest to him. And Jeff is left all alone with the demons of pornography.

Although this is a fictional example, you could probably assign this to 70 percent of boys ages thirteen to eighteen growing up in the church today. Maybe more. According to Jerry Ropelato, more than 80 percent of boys ages thirteen to eighteen are watching hard-core porn.[2]

That's how addiction works.

You become convinced that you can manage your sin, whatever that sin is, and it leads to ultimate isolation.

Think about all the overdose cases you read about on the news. Do you think for a second that the person has any desire to overdose? Do you think there's anyone who wants to wake up as a meth addict with no teeth, no hair, and skin that looks like fifty-year-old, dried-out leather? Of course not.

Drug addiction isn't a mysterious addiction. There's no rocket science to it. We know addictions are simply long stints of behavioral events usually kept secret that always lead to isolation.

And don't be fooled.

Porn is an addiction.

Drugs are an addiction.

Sexual relationships can be an addiction.

Food can be an addiction.

Now, hold on to your hats . . .

Family can be an addiction.

Friendships can be an addiction.

Church can be an addiction.

And all, when taken to the extreme, can work themselves into dangerous isolations.

Church? Church can't be an addiction, you say.

How many people have an unhealthy addiction to being at, working for, volunteering with, or providing for a local church? Our churches are filled with people who think that if they grace the threshold every Sunday and Wednesday, they've not only helped out the community but are doing divine work. They have tied God's happiness to a work of volunteering, and that's just not how God works.

God is pleased.

He's pleased with humanity.

He's so pleased that the Bible says, "God so loved the world" (John 3:16). But don't stop at verse 16; move on to verse 17, which says, "God did not send his Son into the world to condemn the world, but to save the world through him."

Even in our addictions that are justified as healthy, we serve a God who loves us, cares for us, and wants us to know Him in a real way. He doesn't qualify the people He allows to the throne room. He already took care of that.

When Jesus came to die on the cross and be raised from the dead, the whole of humanity took a different form. The consequences of breaking the law were mitigated to grace, and sin was defeated.

Sure, there are still bad things that happen in the world today, but just read the Scriptures when they refer to the importance of Jesus' work here on earth. The shame and guilt associated with addiction needs to be erased. Jesus didn't come so we could live in the consequences of our poor decision making; He came so we might have life, and life more abundantly (see John 10:10).

So no matter your sin, your addiction, the thing you go back to in order to find peace and comfort, God is in the business of forgiving that sin and cleansing you from all unrighteousness (see 1 John 1:9).

CHAPTER 8

LOOKING FOR LOVE IN ALL THE WRONG PLACES

AS MY GIRLS were growing up, we bought into the Dream of Disney. We bought them every movie with a princess in it, thinking all along that the princess dream would build self-confidence and give them dreams to dream about when life got hard.

There's no doubt that Disney is the best at what they do. If you go to the theme parks, they are clean, well run, and best in class. If you watch television, the Disney/ABC Television Group has some of the finest programming around. Even in their movie distribution businesses, Buena Vista, Disney is in a class all their own.

But this princess story, I'm not so sure about.

Take the priceless story of Cinderella, for example. The daughter of an evil stepmother, with two evil stepsisters, lives in the dark shadowy hallways of slavery in her own family. Cinderella is the epitome of lonely.

She is forced to sweep the house while the others go out and have fun.

Her only friends are the rats of the home.

Her sisters are constantly telling her what to do because she doesn't belong to the same class they do.

For the whole first half of the story, we are longing for Cinderella to rise up and give the sisters a swift kick in the behind, but we linger with her as she mopes around doing the household chores. What a picture of alone.

Then the fairy godmother arrives. She turns Cinderella into an attractive princess, dead set on going to the ball where her evil stepsisters think they will meet the handsome prince.

The angelic godmother gives Cinderella a few rules, and off she goes to the party to impress the locals, embarrass her sisters, and ultimately win the affection of the handsome prince.

And all this is taught to our kids before they reach puberty.

Now, don't get me wrong, I'm not writing a book to knock Disney.

I'm not trying to demolish the hopes and dreams that someday, with a little help, the ugly duckling (another great bedtime tale we teach our kids) will turn into the beautiful princess. But think about it.

The moral of the story is . . .

If you look pretty, you'll be accepted.

If you impress the class of important people, your life will be all right.

If you just hide the *real* you, you'll find success.

Looking back on it, I wonder if we haven't created generations of girls who can't understand why they don't matter. They continually find themselves in the dark dirty home washing dishes and doing housework and that *can't be* success.

(Please don't read any feminism into that comment. Boys have the same issues here as girls.)

If taken literally, the Cinderella story gives us few keys to being okay in the skin we were created in.

CLIQUES

I don't know if you've ever seen the movie *Mean Girls*, but so many of us live inside this world.

There are popular girls and not popular girls.

The popular ones are the ones who have life all together.

They are the cheerleaders, the ones with boyfriends, and the ones who dress to the nines.

They find safety when they establish a group that keeps others out.

If you're in the clique, it seems as though life is good.

You have a certain group of friends you can call by name.

You have someone to call and someone to text.

You know that someone will have your back when the world starts to fall apart.

On the outside, it seems as though everything is well.

But we know the outside doesn't always reveal the truth, right?

A couple of months ago, I was talking to a friend who goes to college. She's struggled to make friends, but on the outside, she gave the impression that all was going well. She seemed to be connected to a group of friends who had fun together, went out on the weekends, and stayed up late studying together.

One night they were all getting ready to go out on the town and my friend was walking down the hallway of their dorm. She was excited, her mind filled with stories they were about to make together, when another girl walked into the hallway and said, "Hey!"

My friend naturally responded, "Hey, how are you?" and that was the end of the conversation, just two people exchanging friendly acknowledgments.

Fast-forward a couple of hours later.

All the girls were heading home from the restaurant where they'd just spent a couple of hours sharing life stories together, when one of the girls asked, "What were you talking to that other girl about?"

My friend answered, "Oh, it was nothing. I just saw her and said hey."

The driver of the car stopped the car in the middle of the highway and told my friend to get out.

"What's wrong?" she asked.

"That's the girl who was flirting with my boyfriend yesterday. If you want to hang out with us, you can't hang out with her," the driver answered.

"We weren't hanging out. I just said hey," my friend retorted.

"Look, that's it. If you want to be with us, you can't be with her."

And they dropped my friend off on the highway, miles from the school.

And that's what cliques look like.

There are unwritten rules in a group like that where it seems as though safety in numbers would be a benefit.

It seems like the others would have your back, no matter the cost. But evidently when you cross a certain line, you get thrown to the curb (in my friend's case, quite literally). And then the feelings of rejection, worthlessness, and loneliness begin to creep in.

So many times we want to find security, but at what cost?

CRIME

Another friend of mine found significance from taking things when he walked through retail stores. He would walk inside a department store and see something he wanted. Ever thought to yourself, *I could take this and no one would know*? It's more common than you think.

According to the National Learning and Resource Center, one in eleven people is a shoplifter. More than 10 million people have been caught shoplifting each year, which equals more than $13 billion of goods stolen from retailers each year.[1]

Why do people begin shoplifting?

What makes us want to take something we don't own?

I talk to shoplifters and find that most of them can afford the goods they steal, but having something they can control fills a gap somewhere in the brain. It's a strange phenomenon on the outside, but inside you begin taking steps to justify illegal behavior to fill the hole of acceptance in your heart.

For the shoplifter who gets caught, the consequences involve going to jail! But for the shoplifter who doesn't get caught, the synapses in the brain that are temporarily satisfied long for more. Stealing—with its excitement, fear, and satisfaction—becomes an addictive cycle that fills the gap of pain. Some might even say that they find meaning when they shoplift.

It's just another process in which pain can be covered up with something on the outside but not the inside.

SEX

I met Allen when he was a sophomore in high school. He's a tall, good-looking guy who was obviously the whisper of all the girl circles.

Somehow I could just tell.

Allen came to me at a conference with his head held low. I had just finished a seminar on teen sex and dating in which my main point is that sex is just the veneer of something else going on inside of humanity.

We can talk about the ills of the teenage world all we want, but the truth is that sex, drugs, and rock and roll have been around for a long time. There are multitudes of nonprofits interested in addressing the veneer of issues. I want to ask a new question: *Why?*

Why is sex such a pervasive undercurrent in our lives?

Whether it's the draw to pornography, the need to joke in a sexual way, or—let's just come right out and say it—the desire to engage in risky sexual activity . . . why?

Sure it might be biology.

It might be the culture around us forcing us to think a certain way.

It might even be attributed to the way boys or girls around us are dressed.

But it doesn't answer the question.

Unless we are just designed to populate the planet, and the hormonal age of heightened awareness is in our teenage years, why are so many kids having sex?

But back to Allen.

He held his head low as he confessed having multiple sex partners over the last year. He was feeling guilty and shameful because he realized that we all have a responsibility to care for our own sexuality and for the sexuality of those around us.

"Andy, I just don't know what to think anymore."

I could tell he was lost.

Each sexual partner Allen chose gave him a sense of meaning

for a short time, but the need for more overcame him on a daily basis, and he was longing to find meaning in his sexuality.

There's a reason God designed sexual relationships to be confined to marriage. It's not as though God saw an opportunity to engage in a cosmic joke by injecting the teenage population with an insatiable amount of sexual hormones and then leaning over to the angels with a smirk, "Now watch this!"

"DON'T HAVE SEX!"

No, the reason God designed sexuality the way He did was to help people engage in a relationship at the most vulnerable level. It was designed so we could feel love. And now it's been reduced to a hook-up.

Finding love through sexuality outside the boundaries of a committed marriage relationship never works.

There's always more.

Just go back and read the history of people addicted to sex.

It's not the sex they desire; it's the feeling of love and acceptance.

It's a pain on the inside being satisfied by physical touch on the outside.

That's why Allen felt empty inside. He couldn't find satisfaction through sex anymore. And I know a lot of people just like Allen.

ABUSE

I was driving down the road the other day and heard a song by Eminem on the radio. Now, whether you think Eminem is a genius or the devil incarnate, the words to the song "Love the Way You Lie" speak to the pain of abuse and how it fills our need to feel loved.

It seems sick on the outside, but on the inside, I know this world. I've heard the stories of women who wake up every day and look for a way out but for some reason find love in the middle of an abusive relationship. The psyche doesn't allow the victim to see reality, and the cloud of confusion and unworthiness begins to cover what is really going on.

Abuse is an addiction.

Abuse can be covering up the hole of pain.

It can help us get through the day.

In a sick way, it makes us feel as though we are alive.

But the abusive relationships I see never end up good. Unless the victim finds another way to meet that need, the abuser wins and often winds up hurting both of them in the process.

THE ONLY WAY TO FILL THE GAP

So why?

Why are we so inclined to fill our lives with things that can never validate us?

In many ways, validation is the cure to loneliness. Understanding the human condition means understanding our need for validation.

But drugs don't validate you.

Sex doesn't validate you.

Addiction doesn't validate you.

When you try to fill this need on your own, it only leads to temptation and sin. In James we read, "Each person is tempted when they are dragged away by their own evil desire and enticed. Then, after desire has conceived, it gives birth to sin; and sin, when it is full-grown, gives birth to death" (1:14-15).

Isn't it interesting how shiny temptation looks on the outside?

You begin justifying: *I need this. No one will know. I'm not hurting anyone else*. But after we are enticed to do something outside the boundaries of God's will, we find ourselves in a place that leads to death.

The only way the human condition can truly be satisfied is by understanding who the Creator of the universe is. Then, after we discover the Creator, we have an obligation to see His reason and purpose for our lives.

Once we realize He knew us in the beginning . . .

He knows the number of hairs on our heads . . .

He knows the number of days we are going to live . . .

Once we believe that, the hole starts filling.

It's the whole reason Jesus gave the Greatest Commandment in Matthew 22.

It's the reason God created us in communion from the beginning.

Jesus knew the addition of loving others was crucial to understanding how God works on the planet.

Jesus was giving the Pharisees the beginning of understanding. He was giving them a picture of whole living. He laid out the secret to knowing how to love others and fill the hole and longing with what truly matters.

We can look for love in all the wrong places, but when we finally give in and begin loving God with everything, when we learn what it means to choose to love those around us, the hole begins to fill.

We learn what it means to love ourselves in the moment.

We learn what it means to see how God sees us.

We understand that the Creator of the universe is interested in us.

Some might see faith as a crutch, but really we're all living with a crutch of some sort. If you decide that you can fill the hole of loneliness with anything but the love and peace of God, you are in essence choosing a crutch to get yourself through this world.

You have to ask yourself what good it does to spin your wheels on all these other things.

I've never met a drug addict satisfied with his or her addiction.

I've never met someone looking for love through sex completely satisfied.

I've never met someone enduring abuse finding peace.

Everyone on the planet is doing the best they can with what they've got.

But if He is real, if God is who He claims to be in the Scriptures, if He is the God who claims to have formed me in my mother's inmost womb, what do I have to lose?

If you're looking for significance in anything else, take a chance on a God who spun the planets into existence. Consider a God who hurled the stars into the sky. Consider a God who told the waves when to stop and the storms when to calm. He is the only One who can turn the pain of longing into satisfaction.

CHAPTER 9

REAL MEN

THE CONVERSATION IS everywhere. Whether you're asking in the context of school, a job, or just a social event, "What is a man?" is on the lips of many.

Is a man someone who likes *Braveheart*, beats his chest, and hunts with a bow and arrow?

Is a man someone who can cry at Hallmark commercials without being embarrassed?

Is a man someone who can look at the world and declare his individuality in the face of conformity?

Or is a man something totally different?

Western culture has long used images of cowboys, warriors, and even professional athletes to garner the iconic manhood that many are trying to become. John Wayne, William Wallace, and a 250-pound middle linebacker who plays for the Green Bay Packers are surely men, right? But what if you don't fit into any of those categories? Does it lead us males into an abyss of insecurity?

Each summer, we see almost five hundred teenage boys at our Adventure facility in Durango. We named it KIVU after a long hard debate over what teenagers are looking for today. Kivu is actually the sixth-largest lake in Rwanda and in the native tongue means "big." So the lake in the northern part of the small African country is literally called "big lake."

We wanted to invite a population of teenagers to something *big*.

Big adventure.

Big experience.

Big fun.

Big relationship building and networking.

But most important, we wanted a safe haven where boys weren't afraid to go big with their manhood.

During the inception of the camp, one of my leaders asked if we could have some time where the guys could be away from the rest of the group to just act like guys.

"Look, no offense," he started, "but worship music is turning into something of a love song to my imaginary Jesus lover rather than encouraging men to be men. What if we had a place where the guys could express themselves however they wanted?"

I agreed. And the Alamo was born.

At the Alamo, the guys have a chance to talk through some of the issues they are trying to reconcile culturally. They also let off a lot of steam. They blow stuff up, beat on broken vehicles, yell and scream, and all the while develop deep connections of what it means to be a man in today's culture.

REAL MEN OF THE BIBLE

Remember the story of Moses and Joshua?

Moses led the Israelites out of Egypt in the Exodus story, but during the transfer of power, when Moses was coming to the end of his life, he appointed Joshua to take over and lead the people into the Promised Land.

Joshua 1 is one of the manliest chapters in the Bible because Joshua has to look into the heart of being a leader of a nation and stand up to his fears. Only then can he lead the people into the promise God had for them.

"Be strong and courageous," it says over and over in the book of Joshua as God tries to encourage the new leader to face fear, overcome insecurity, and go out to lead. If ever there was a template for what it takes to be a man, I think Joshua gives it to us.

It doesn't matter if they're football players or artists, *all men* can resonate with the call of God in Joshua's life. So as we take a look at the question "What is a man?" I propose we begin eliminating the areas in our lives where manliness fades away.

FEAR

One of the most common components of manhood confusion is the fear factor. Have you ever watched the popular show that invites people to overcome their fear of heights, their fear of snakes, or even their fear of food?

It's amazing to watch men and women from all walks of life try to figure out how to convince their psyche to engage in something that seems so naturally scary. I think the popularity of this show can be attributed to the fact that we are all scared of that stuff.

I've watched grown NFL players cry when they get up on a high ropes course. I've seen women flip out when they have to face their fear of mice. I've watched some of the smartest men in the world have issues when they see a little spider spinning a web in their corner offices.

The power of fear over our lives is amazing.

When God called Joshua to lead the nation of Israel to the Promised Land, it's no coincidence He called him to be courageous. Fear is a part of who we are.

We were made to look into the shadow of fear in our lives and take direction.

We were fashioned to take risks and experience success on the other side.

For whatever reason, every man, no matter what gifts God gave him, was given the DNA to be a little scared on the forefront of decisions, calculate the cost, and then dive in headfirst to overcome.

How can I prove it?

Spend some time with elementary-age boys. Ask them, "What do you want to be when you grow up?" You'll get a list a mile long.

I want to be a fireman.

I want to be a policeman.

I want to be a doctor.

I want to be an army ranger.

I want to be a cowboy.

I want to be a pilot.

I want to be an astronaut.

All of the professions young boys dream of include some sort of calculated risk—the ability to live on the edge.

No kid ever says he wants to be an investment banker.

No kid ever says he wants to sit in an office cubicle all day long.

None of the kids aspires to run a retail store.

Of course, all of these professions contain elements of risk and adventure, but it's interesting to note how drastically those ideas change.

Why do so many men grow up and change their minds?

Maybe it's because we live in a culture where there are so many ways to make a living that the gifts given to us can span many industries.

Maybe it's because we learn how to tame our risk calculations as we go through our education system.

Maybe it's just trying to grow up and live responsibly in a Western culture.

Or maybe it's because we've replaced the idea of risk and adventure with the idea of wealth and comfort.

Loneliness begins to creep into a man's life when adventure and risk are taken out of the equation, when men have to replace their God-given desires with something "more responsible." I've seen men who go to work without purpose and ask themselves, "What good is my life?" I've interviewed men in their final years of life who look back with regret because they opted for something more comfortable rather than taking the risk of adventure in their early years.

Why else are men attracted to movies of adventure, mystery, and intrigue? The *Pirates of the Caribbean* movies have grossed hundreds of millions of dollars, and very rarely do I talk to women where Jack Sparrow is on the top-ten of their favorite characters. Johnny Depp, maybe, but it's primarily men who identify with Jack Sparrow the pirate. Why?

Could it be that the ability to look adventure in the face and overcome fear is woven inside men at the core level?

Could it be that the need to feel "alive" is something all men long for?

Could it be that all men can stand behind the character Jack Sparrow embodies, the everyman character in his search for hidden treasure, the rescue of the fair maiden, and the warped sense of justice?

Men need to sense that what they are doing in the world is courageous. They need to feel the sense of responsibility and freedom. They need to have opportunities to express their manhood.

Unfortunately, we've focused so much on creating "civil" men in our culture that we've emasculated men to be easier to deal with rather than allowing men to be men.

Allowing "boys to be boys" is a good way for guys to overcome the fear of circumstance, and they can create an environment where they can relate to other men. Our little slice of manliness, the Alamo, is somewhere teenage boys can overcome the fear of being a man. They can see a place where being a man is celebrated rather than tamed. They have the opportunity to express their desire to be a leader and face their fears, all in the context of biblical principles.

We encourage our boys to stand up and be men.

We help them overcome their fear of looking silly when they talk to girls.

We help them see the value and valor of doing the right thing.

They get a chance to be mentored by other men who've found keys to loving God in the context of being manly.

We've lifted the shroud of cultural identity, and we've allowed for boys to join the elite group of manhood.

Do you have a place where men can be men?

If not, I invite you to create an arena where the cultural pressures of being a man can fade and you can feel the freedom to be what God created you to be.

PURPOSE

The second key to lifting loneliness out of manhood is to give men a sense of purpose. We're living in a world where only a special few get to experience the value of their work in school or the workplace. Unless you're a football star, scholar, or executive, you're usually held to a more ordinary "worker"-level position. I believe that all men need a sense of purpose. They need to know their work matters.

Sometimes purpose can be an illusory term. I remember working for a man in the video-store business. (I know, this really shows my age.) Back in the eighties and nineties, when companies such as Blockbuster were making millions on the rentals of VHS tapes and DVDs, renting movies was the only way somebody could see a movie without going to the theater.

We didn't have iTunes.

We didn't have Hulu or Netflix.

We didn't even have Redbox.

You had to drive down to your local video-store rental facility and check out a movie, like you would a book at the library.

In any event, I remember checking in movies, checking out movies, suggesting the latest titles to customers. One day I met with my boss in the back office.

"Andy, I need you to take every movie off the shelf and put all the titles in this new box." He devised a plan to save money on the normal boxes we used and basically restructure the business to be more customer friendly.

"You know that's going to take *a long time*, right? I mean, we have over five thousand titles in this store alone."

"Just do it."

And off I went. I took down the oldest movies first and started implementing the system my boss devised.

Looking back, I can see why he decided to change the system. It was easier to do it the new way. It was more cost effective to do it the new way. It made more sense from a customer point of view.

But I was seventeen years old, and I had no idea why in the world I needed to spend my time recreating a system that was working.

I started thinking to myself . . .

Couldn't we just phase in the system?

What if we decided to keep the movies in the back room and let people see only posters of the movies?

What if we combined the systems for a short time so you could get double the work out of me for the same price?

It didn't matter.

The boss said this is the way we're doing it, so that's the way we did it.

It was like all the times my mother told me to do something. I asked why and she looked back at me with those mother eyes and demanded, "Because I'm your mother, that's why."

At seventeen, I found myself feeling very insecure. I knew what to do, but at the time, I didn't know why I was doing it. There was a cloud of confusion because my boss hadn't taken the time to tell me what he was up to. The purpose of the system change was clear in his mind, but the one who was responsible for implementing it had no idea what benefit this had to the overall company.

I realize it's hard to communicate in business. It's probably one of the core issues most companies face on a day-to-day basis. How to bring people into the conversation is a tough job, and that's why CEOs make the big bucks.

But this isn't only a problem in business.

Have you ever sat in class wondering, *Why am I learning this? I will never use this in my whole life.*

Yeah, me too.

I had to take a history class focused on the point of view of major American feminism. I learned a lot about the women who helped found the country, but I was a performance major. How in the world was that supposed to relate to my theater degree?

I felt as though I had no purpose in that class.

Purposelessness in manhood leads to insecurity.

Insecurity leads to anxiousness.

Anxiousness starts driving in the dark clouds of loneliness.

And before long, men are wondering if their lives even matter.

In adolescents, this is the origin of many suicide decisions. Somehow, a young man walking through life comes to a crossroads of purpose, and the decision to cease existing is just a toss-up.

Men struggling with suicidal thoughts have come to the conclusion that death is a better way out of their situation than sticking to their guns. They see no reason to keep going. Be it relational problems, vocational problems, or even inner turmoil, the place where taking one's own life becomes a solution is a purposeless place.

Men need purpose.

We need places where we know where we're going and why.

Whether we're sitting at a desk in a crowded schoolroom or walking through the campus at an Ivy League school, we need to know that where we are going and the time it takes to get there are valuable.

TOGETHERNESS

Let's just get right to it: Relationships are hard for most men.

We don't want to be seen as vulnerable.

We have no desire to show our weaknesses.

We're not very adept at reaching out to find out what makes someone else tick.

We're selfish.

We sense the need to conquer.

All of our heroes stand on the mountaintop alone as if they got there all by themselves.

Somewhere we've been taught that a man is someone who can pull his life together by his bootstraps and make it.

Someone has whispered in our ears that a true man can do it on his own.

And I've gotta be honest right here: This is me.

For the longest time, I felt as if my responsibility to the world was to raise myself to a position where others would give me praise. Whether it was in academics, performance, athletics, or even relationships, I needed others to see that I mattered and could handle it.

I have friends in the same situation.

Their aloneness happens when life begins to fall apart. It's not really anything of their own doing, but when circumstances begin to dictate their ability to be the man on top of the mountain, they start to feel alone.

Phrases like "If only I could . . ." or "It's not my fault; they should have . . ."

Sometimes I hear men say things like "I just didn't have what it takes . . ."

Somewhere in their own wounded history, they were told that if you can't do it on your own, it's not worth doing. But I believe that nothing could be further from God's plan for manhood on the planet today.

If our value is tied to whatever we can do, it has to be tied to the times we can't. Success and failure are circumstances in and out of our control. However, when purpose is at the center of our existence, we're halfway there.

We need to feel that it's okay to be men and count on each other—where we can explore something together, conquer something as one, and be validated as men.

We need to give something to achieve a goal, and we need to be part of something bigger than ourselves.

Yet if we can just learn to trust God's plan, that we're all in this together, that sometimes our purpose is just to lift each other up, then every day, every moment, every breath has a purpose.

We may not see it now and, like Joshua, we may not know the entire plan.

But isn't that part of the adventure?

CHAPTER 10

REAL WOMEN

RIGHT ABOUT NOW you might be thinking, *Is this guy for real? He's going to tell* me *what it's like to be a girl today and how I should feel?*

I confess, those thoughts crossed my mind too. But I've talked with quite a few girls and women over the years, and my wife has helped me understand a lot more than I ever could on my own, so I'm going to take a stab at shedding some light on a few things.

I know, too, that even by attempting to write a chapter called "Real Women," there will be people attacking from all sides. Conservative Christian circles will point to the Bible as the guide to the role of a woman, and I don't disagree! The Bible is full of incredible examples of women and how God sees them. But often the role we see cast (taken from portions of Scripture) feels like a walk-on part on a sitcom with no character development. We hear descriptions like . . .

A real woman is a wife and mother (or aspires to be).

Women should run the home and be industrious and servant-minded.

Liberal circles will take issue with the fact that I even reference the Bible in a gender debate, noting women's rights to work, preach, and be as equal as any man under any circumstance.

I get it.

This is going to be controversial.

But I'm not writing just to stir the pot.

I'm writing in hopes that you can understand your purpose in this crazy, pushy, high-pressure world.

JUMPING THROUGH HOOPS, LANDING IN A HOLE

The other day, I turned on the television to let my brain relax.

You ever do that?

Do you ever find yourself tired of everything going on around you so you turn on the TV, go to watch a movie, or just sit and watch YouTube videos for a while?

I guess there are enough people who sit around looking for an escape that DIRECTV can continue adding channels to its lineup. Flipping through the channels, I found over two hundred stations.

Two hundred?! What do we need two hundred channels for?

In any event, I was flipping through the channels and it seemed that every show and commercial on TV had something to say about gender issues. While some pushed the boundaries of typical stereotypes, others were fueled by them.

Women are either homemakers or they're trying to find their love interests in romantic comedies.

Guys are the strong hero types, out saving the day.

Girls are portrayed as sex symbols, wearing less and less.

The commercials tell an even more intriguing picture . . .

Men are taking control of their banking problems.

Women are sweeping the kitchen.

Men are driving the newest car being released next year.

Women are paraded around on a beach in skimpy bikinis.

Men are conquering.

Women are helping.

I guess there are a few examples where a woman goes out to conquer, but I think, at least on the day I was watching, they were the exception to the rule rather than the rule. And even when women were the ones saving the day, they did it in their designer clothes with perfect hair and makeup.

So what gives?

According to TV (and the media in general), girls are supposed to be humorous and sexy enough to attract the cute guy, be strong (but not *too* strong), have the brains and the charisma to carry on witty conversations, be fashionable, and, let's not forget, do all of that while maintaining the perfect hair, makeup, and body.

Talk about pressure!

No wonder so many girls today feel alone. How can one person possibly live up to all those expectations?

I've talked to countless girls over the years who truly believe that if they can just date the right guy or become popular or excel in school, they'll find the recognition and acceptance they so desperately want. But the feelings of worthlessness these girls are already experiencing only deepen as they seek to keep the boyfriend's attention with sex, lose their individuality by trying to fit in with the in crowd, or isolate themselves by spending all their free time on homework.

So what are you supposed to do?

How can you find your role in society today?

How are you supposed to know what your natural purpose is?

And what if you already know what your passions are but everyone and everything around you says you're wrong?

THE TROUBLE WITH LABELS

I've heard so many pastors, youth leaders, and even some communities label people generically so as to help others find their identities. Don't get me wrong: It's helpful to have a starting place as we try to figure out how to fit in, but so many times the boundaries we set for certain genders are too tight.

As you know firsthand, girls are expected to act a certain way. But when one comes along and says, "Well, I just don't find joy in doing ____________," often we point her back to a Bible verse, a community tradition, or some sort of line in the sand we drew so we could be comfortable with women's roles.

I was talking with a student in a Christian school not long ago. She was wrestling with the idea of becoming a doctor, but she also wanted to be a mom and have a good husband.

Someone in her life was telling her, "God designed you to be a good wife. There's no way you can be both a good doctor and a good wife."

Really?

Women can't explore their own dreams and ideas, lest they challenge the way God created them to be at home?

What if we've got it all wrong?

What if gender roles don't do anything more than lock people into stereotypes they don't fit?

I find it incredibly difficult to understand the pressure girls today face, primarily because I'm not a woman, but I truly believe many girls just feel trapped. Or worse, they find themselves trying to be like the women their peer groups say are perfect.

The next time you're at a magazine stand, look at the images of women on the front cover of *women's* magazines.

They're not real.

They're not honest with who they are.

They've been airbrushed and Photoshopped, and many have undergone several cosmetic surgeries to look like they do.

And somehow we expect you to grow up without identity issues?

There's no way.

Even women exploit women for product sales.

We've set up a system that eats itself from the inside, and we (the generations before you) have failed you.

From talking with many of you, I know that today's girls feel that they have so much more to offer the world than their looks or the part they play in romantic relationships. But you often find yourselves in a role—dictated often by men, sometimes by women themselves—in which you can't fully express your gifts. I find there are wonderfully gifted people forced into being something because they're "supposed" to be that way.

So how can knowing your purpose and pursuing it actually help take away the loneliness? And where can you find this purpose and freedom?

CHASING TRUTH

As you grow older, you're probably going to learn what your purpose is from the three biggest influences in your life: your family, your friends, and the media around you.

So what happens if your parents don't seem to care? Or don't know? Or they're telling you the same things you see on TV all the time?

What if your friends seem to be your friends only because of the clothes you wear or the guy you date?

What if you, and the people around you, are equally influenced by the images and messages of the media?

Where can you turn to find the truth about your purpose?

I mentioned it before, and I'm hoping you'll hear me out. The best place for finding truth is in God's Word.

Not long ago, I was teaching basic Christian worldview principles to a group in Minnesota. I was working through the issues of God, purpose, and mankind, when a girl in the front row raised her hand.

"Look, I'm all for hope. I'm all for finding purpose," she said. "But isn't the Bible just a book written by men, for men, and extremely male-centric? I don't like the idea that women are just supposed to sit beside their man. What if I don't ever get married? Where do I fit into the story?"

It kind of took me aback.

The girl was fourteen years old and obviously struggling with the boundaries of the gender roles being taught in her life. I went back to my hotel and really starting thinking about this.

Was she feeling boxed in at home? At youth group? At church? What exactly had she been taught that the Bible says about women? And is there room for us to understand the time period in which the Bible was written?

You see, the thing we have to remember about the Bible is that it was written in a time when, culturally, women were seen as little more than property—not very valuable. But Western civilization has pushed the boundaries for the roles of women far beyond what Paul and the other writers ever thought could happen. Think about it: Women have had the right to vote in the general democratic system here in America for only the last one hundred years.

So how can we reconcile what was written then with what God has planned for women now?

If you grow up your whole life hearing you're supposed to cook and clean in the kitchen, it doesn't give you very much room to dream, especially if God created you for something different.

And I think a lot of girls' feelings of loneliness happen when they believe they have to fit a specific mold of expectations and stereotypes without allowing room to breathe outside the walls our culture and communities have created.

Many girls sit inside the traditional values they've been taught and think that if they don't line up like that, there's something wrong with them. I've even seen some girls push the boundaries of gender roles to prove people wrong and then find themselves out on a limb with no support.

What if we could read between the lines of the Bible and know what, besides the list of virtues in Proverbs 31, a real woman can be in God's eyes?

FINDING ENCOURAGEMENT

It's no secret that girls are looking for significance as much as guys are.

So how can you see yourself in the trans-biblical story and understand God's incredible love and purpose for you?

You might have heard there are passages in the Bible that point to a man's role being the head of the household. There are places where Paul writes of strict roles of women in the church. But when was the last time you heard of Jesus' view of women?

Would you be surprised to know that Jesus was a revolutionary looking to elevate the status of women in a culture where women were seen as objects?

Remember when Jesus decided to walk through Samaria to get to a location where He could preach? Remember the woman who happened to be at the side of the well gathering water for her family? Remember what Jesus decided to do?

You can read the whole story in John 4. Jesus happens upon Jacob's well and meets a Samaritan woman ready to draw water. He initiates conversation with her and in the end reveals His divinity.

Men weren't supposed to even talk to women they didn't know in that day.

Jewish Rabbis weren't in the business of engaging in conversation with Samaritans.

There's no way the culture would understand the Savior's revealing His identity to a woman. This woman had been married five times, and she was living with a man who wasn't her husband, and Jesus sits down and allows her in on the universe's biggest secret since the Creation.

It's one of the most touching stories in the New Testament because Jesus saw in this woman the gift of sharing. He knew she would go back and care for the people in her community so much that she would be willing to share the water that He gives.

Remember?

He said, "Everyone who drinks this water will be thirsty again, but whoever drinks the water I give them will never thirst. Indeed, the water I give them will become in them a spring of water welling up to eternal life" (John 4:13-14).

Why would God, if He intended to put strict boundaries on gender roles, entrust this sinful woman to sharing His secret with the rest of the town?

Why would He even offer this honor to someone He thought should be in the kitchen cooking dinner?

Could it be that Jesus saw something interesting in the heart of this woman?

Could it be He insisted she use her gifts for the benefit of all mankind?

Could it be Jesus knew how to encourage this woman to be a part of a new global history?

He didn't tell her, "Now go be a good girl."

He didn't patronize her by saying, "If you just do what your husband says . . ."

He didn't try to put her in her place with false rules and regulations.

Jesus invited the woman at the well into the greatest story ever told. He valued her. He sensed, despite her sin, there was good. He knew that if He took time with her, an entire community would change. He gave us a picture of how God wants to encourage girls and women in the world today.

THE MOST IMPORTANT REVELATION

Think back to Jesus' friendship with Mary and Martha.

Remember when His friend (their brother) Lazarus died and the pain was so overwhelming that the Bible says, "Jesus wept" (John 11:35)? You can read the story in John 11.

The friendship Jesus established with these women was more than a hospitality type of friendship. He didn't simply desire they serve Him every time He passed by their house. No, I believe that Jesus cared deeply for these women. He cared so much that it pained Him when their loved one passed away.

Remember who Jesus appeared to first when He walked out of the grave?

Don't overlook this.

In the day and age when a woman's opinion in the court of law was seen as less than impeccable, the most important event in all of human history was first revealed to a woman!

It would be a woman who ran to Peter to announce the risen Savior.

It would be a woman who carried the secret of God's great mystery.

It was a woman who God entrusted with the most important event in all of history.

Girls, God loves you!

He doesn't want you to sit in the dark corners of the world picking up after the failures of men.

He doesn't desire that you bow to some subversive role in the world.

He cares for you deeply and has given you a special gift to be seen by those you interact with.

A REAL WOMAN'S VALIDITY IN GOD'S EYES

So many girls and women today are trying to find validation in the way their bodies are shaped.

So many are holding on to a dream of marriage or romantic-comedy ideals of what women are.

So many of you are forgetting you have a valuable gift, a gift that God gave you specifically to use so we can see the whole of the body of Christ in perfect action.

Culture's whole idea of a real woman is a farce.

There's no such thing.

There is no perfect girlfriend.

There is no perfect employee.

There is no perfect friend.

There is no perfect body type or student or athlete.

There's no such thing as a perfect woman who finds the perfect role for her perfect situation.

Those who continue to assign a high value to that mythical person who has it all together are driving themselves mad with the idea that they can achieve her. It's from this feeling of failure, of never measuring up, that the loneliness sets in.

Don't you see? That perfect girl? She's not real! Once you are able to die to that need for perfection, you can begin to identify where you fit in best.

For many of you, you'll be called to be a good friend.

For some of you, being at home, raising kids, and working on keeping the family together will be your calling.

For others, being the CEO of a major multinational corporation suits your gifts better.

For some, you are called to share your hospitality.

For others of you, God needs you to be out in the world being doctors, lawyers, small-business owners, astronauts, and everything in between.

My hope is that as you search for the gift God gave you, you will be able to find someone in your life to encourage you to be the best *you* that you can be.

There's no magic mold.

There are no expectations.

There are no boundaries.

God made you unique and expects important things from you. As you come to know and understand the validation He gave women throughout Scripture, I pray that you will know that He loves you.

So break the mold, tear off the labels, and smash the box you are in. When we, guys or girls, are doing what God uniquely created us to do, we can find a harmony in the togetherness of working as one unit for Him.

CHAPTER 11

REAL JOY

Grief can take care of itself, but to get the full value of a joy, you must have somebody to divide it with.

— Mark Twain

Rejoice in the Lord always. I will say it again: Rejoice!

— Philippians 4:4

LANGUAGE IS SUCH a funny thing.

Words we use are so important.

Phrases we say, the tone we say them in, and the context of a word can really throw someone for a loop.

Some words are hard to understand, mainly because we just don't use them in today's world.

Sometimes when I ask a student to pray, I get something like this:

> Dear Gracious Heavenly Father,
>
> Please bestow upon us the blessings of Your hand. May we partake of Your ever loving kindness, and may this food bring nourishment to our bodies. Amen.

Out of respect, I keep my eyes closed and my hands folded but often find myself chuckling underneath my breath at the sheer confusion of the string of words I just heard.

How many times do we use this language in real life?

Bestow? What does it even mean?

I looked it up. Webster's has several meanings:

1. To put to use
2. To put in a particular or appropriate place
3. To provide with quarters
4. To convey as a gift—usually used with *on* or *upon*[1]

And what about "partaking of Your ever loving kindness"? Now that's a doozy. Can you imagine walking through the hallways of your school, passing a guy coming out of the cafeteria, and hearing him say, "Hey, man, have a great day, and partake of my ever loving kindness"?

Umm . . . what?

We just don't use those words anymore. And for whatever reason, when we start talking about spiritual matters, those words are still a part of the list we feel that we have to drum up to be more godlike. I wonder if God looks down on us from heaven and laughs when we try to sound more godly? I mean really. Do you really think God cares if we use the word *partake*, or would He rather we just be ourselves and say, "Here ya go"?

This brought me to consider other words in the Bible that sound strange. When was the last time you heard someone say, "What's up, girl? Are you rejoicing today?"

After all, *joy* isn't even a word we use very much today.

But Paul says, "Rejoice in the Lord always" (Philippians 4:4). How do we rejoice when every day we feel all alone?

It's hard to walk through the shadows of loneliness while reading about biblical people who are always talking about "the joy of the Lord." There's a notion in the Christian community that everyone who believes in God has to have a smile on his or her face all the time. So how do we do that?

WHAT IS JOY?

The first step in understanding true joy is defining what joy actually is.

It's a feeling.

It's an emotion.

It's a state of mind.

It's the ability to know that the desires of your heart are being fulfilled.

It's *not* happiness.

It's *not* the constant state of euphoria.

It's *not* everything lining up perfectly.

It's unrealistic to think that every moment of life is going to be filled with happiness and a feeling that all is right with the world. That's just not the way the world spins. There are times of sadness. There are difficulties we cannot predict. There are moments when everyone has stress and the combination of events of real life invade our world.

We'll get a bad grade on a test.

We'll be in relationships that go wrong.

We'll make mistakes and disappoint those we love.

That's just real life.

So what does it mean to rejoice always?

How can we get to a point where joy becomes a part of our everyday lives?

If we can figure this out, the feelings of loneliness will become less overpowering in our lives and we can rely on confident joy.

We all have a need to be joyful. Every teenager, every college student, every adult has a need to feel validated by someone else; and that makes the foundation of happiness evolve to a state of joyful living.

JOY IS A FUNDAMENTAL PART OF BEING HUMAN

In fact, it's the primary message of the Bible.

From the very beginning, God set Adam and Eve in the Garden of Eden and told them that all creation was theirs for the taking. They could eat from any tree in the garden, with the exception of the Tree of the Knowledge of Good and Evil.

But the garden wasn't the fulfillment of their beings.

It was Genesis 2:18 where God said, "It is not good for the man to be alone." That stands out more than any other description of utopian living. God was saying to Adam, and subsequently to the rest of humanity, "When you try to live alone, it's not good." So God created Eve so man could understand the primary source of joy: togetherness.

What does that look like?

In modern times, joy happens when we interact with each other.

When we see a friend's smile giving us validation that he or she is interested in being with us: joy.

When we hear the words "How are you?" in an honest tone, with honest body language behind it: joy.

When we have an opportunity to rest in the fact that someone else wants us to be the person God created us to be: ultimate joy.

The next question is a logical one: How do we create friendships that will give us joy?

THE JOY OF FRIENDSHIP

Friendship is easy for some people. They understand the natural ebbs and flows of what it takes to develop true, meaningful friendships. It's almost like they were born to make friends. They have an outgoing quality about them, and it's almost like they have the DNA to make friends easily.

I find that the need for teenagers to experience meaningful friendship is vital to their having confidence. We all need to know someone at an authentic level. We need to share life experiences. We need to know what makes someone else matter to the world. And, ultimately, we need to be known by others. I guess that's a main part of friendship: to know and to be known.

So how does this work?

I'll never forget walking into my new junior high school, wondering if I was going to fit in. I transferred across town from a community elementary school, where all my friends lived within a five-mile radius. My parents thought it would be a better educational experience to go to a different school, and although they might have hit the education piece, I was worried about not having any friends.

I'll never forget what it was like to walk into a new school building, see new faces, and wonder if I was ever going to have what it took to impress someone enough to have a friend. I remember going to class and, even though there were several people around me, having a horrible feeling of loneliness in my gut. My heart was lost. My stomach was cramping. My head was spinning. All I wanted to do was go home. I was prepared to convince my parents to let me go back to my old school, with my old friends, back to where they cared about me.

Then one day in the fall, the basketball coach walked through the room and slipped a piece of paper on my desk. It read, "Tryouts today at 3:30."

Basketball was about to start up, and evidently my new school was a basketball school. It seemed as if most of the activities were centered around the basketball schedule, and all the guys were trying out.

I was a little bigger than most kids sitting in my junior high classroom, so I guess the coach thought I might have something to contribute when it came to playing hoops. Little did he know, I wasn't that good and he'd have to spend an extraordinary amount of time teaching me how to play the game.

In any event, when he laid the paper on my desk, one of the guys who sat beside me looked over and asked, "Are you trying out? I can't wait for this."

I smiled at him, and from that moment on, we were best friends.

We carpooled to school together.

Our parents started hanging out together.

We went to school events together and began creating a small group of guys around our friendship.

It was really quite an interesting junior high and high school friendship, and as I think back on how it developed, all it took was one of us willing to share the excitement of tryouts.

CREATING A SAFE PLACE

All friendships start with a safe place. Most of us wonder if anyone will really like us for who we are, so we're always looking for someplace where we can be ourselves without judgment.

When this guy looked over at me and spoke, he offered safety.

Joy begins with a safe place.

The quickest way to initiate friendship is to give people freedom to be themselves. We can't be joyful if we're anxious, fearful, strategizing how to do a better job, or wondering if someone will accept us. If you're interested in beginning a friendship with someone new, you've got to make that person feel as though they can relax. And if someone offers you a safe place to jump in, go for it.

WHAT LANGUAGE ARE YOU SPEAKING?

Interestingly enough, we speak more through our body language than we do through our words. You can imagine what it would have been like had my friend folded his arms and crossed his legs and said, "You ready to join me for basketball tryouts?" followed by a smirk and a grin as if he had an alternate agenda.

Even if his tone had been right and he'd tried to create safety, his body language would have told me something entirely different. The way we represent ourselves to other people is important.

Brain researchers talk about how different parts of the brain work in tandem with each other. First, we see the person who we are going to start a friendship with and read his body language. We size him up. We read his posture to make sure what he is saying is actually lining up with what he's doing. If the left part of our brain checks out, we go to the right side.

The right side of the brain is responsible for language and interpretation. This is where the tone of voice comes into play so quickly. You can say things in different ways to mean certain things, right? Your tone, or the quality of excitement, lays a subtext to what you're doing or what you intend to be doing. So, for example, you might say . . .

"Sure, Mom, I'll get the garbage to the street."

You're smiling.

You move toward the garage.

The sentence is delivered with honesty and excitement.

The tone of your voice is coupled with body language that puts the mother at rest, trusting that you'll do what she's asked you to do.

On another day, you might say, "Sure, Mom, I'll get the garbage to the street."

You're playing your favorite video game.

You say it under your breath.

Your body language is telling Mom that you're more interested in sticking right where you are than finishing the task she just laid on you.

This would be a good example of how those two parts of the brain come into conflict with one another and all of a sudden the peaceful joy vanishes into thin air.

The same principle is true when developing friendships.

While body language speaks volumes, you have to be just as aware of your spoken language. I know it's more fun to speak sarcastically to your friends and make jokes at their expense. And oftentimes there's nothing wrong with laughing together about a poor choice, a funny event, or some sort of blunder that embarrasses someone. But don't be fooled: Every time you poke fun and use sarcasm in a relationship, you're inviting cracks of insecurity to develop. In every well-meaning joke, there's always a little bit of truth.

All I'm saying is that if you're interested in making sure your right brain and your left brain agree with each other, work on your body language, your tone of voice, and the intent of your words. You'll put others at ease, meeting the most fundamental of all human needs both for yourself and someone else.

THE JOY OF RELATIONSHIPS

That's it, isn't it?

Joy isn't getting on the merry-go-round and having a good time.

Joy isn't getting a new cell phone with all the tricks and gadgets.

Joy isn't going on a trip to prove you're somebody.

In fact, joy isn't even meeting someone you idolize to validate your own existence.

Joy is simply this: resting in relationship with God and man.

We've all been around those people who are hard to be around. You know the ones I'm talking about.

They talk a certain way that makes your neck hairs stand up.

They always want something from you.

They demand you do what they want to do.

They have little interest in who you are and how you are developing the gifts God gave you.

Those people are hard to be around.

But there are people we enjoy being around.

They let us be us.

They play video games with us for no other reason than to just hang out.

When you go out to eat, these are the people who you can sit with and almost read their minds and finish their sentences.

This is pure joy.

Wouldn't it be a great testimony to the world if we also found joy in our Maker like that? I think so many people wrestle with the image of God because they've created Him to be some long-bearded CEO who's more interested in corporate profit reports and performance evaluations than just being with us.

They've turned God into this monolithic being, untouchable from the human condition, and we've played right into their hands.

I was at a church not long ago where the worship music was kind of, well, different. The instruments were off-key. The transitions between songs were awkward because the worship leader kept acting as if he were touching porcelain dolls rather than the sweet Taylor guitar he was holding around his neck. Overall, it was just *boring*!

Why do you think some worship services are so boring like that?

I mean, think about it for a minute.

Here we are living in a world created by God.

We worship a God who obviously cares about us, as He's numbered the hairs on our head and the days we're going to live.

We get a chance to bow before Him with our grievances and our requests.

He *listens*.

Even more exciting, *He answers*.

And we want to sing "Just As I Am" as if it's a funeral march down Main Street?

Now, I'm not advocating we all jump ship and describe our faith lives as card-carrying Pentecostals (although many of my friends have found joy in the Lord through the Pentecostal church), but come on.

He's the Creator of all things.

He's the firstborn over all creation.

All things were made by Him and for Him.

He's the head of the church.

He's the head of the body, of which we are all a part.

He hurled the planets into the universe.

He spewed the stars in the sky.

He made all the laws of nature we know to be true today.

He gave us reason and hope to live more abundant lives today!

And all we can do is sway back and forth for fifteen minutes on a Sunday morning and mouth the words to some song of which we don't even know the meaning?

That's not joy.

That's religion.

RELIGION IS NOT RELATIONSHIP

Religion is an obligation.

Religion is a tool to control people.

Religion is a manmade institution masking as God servants.

Religion is process.

Religion is walking a certain amount of steps a day so as to not break the laws set up.

Religion is getting angry when someone reaches out to help someone else in need because it wasn't in the bulletin.

Religion is law without meaning.

Religion is structure without spirit.

It makes people check boxes, and whenever anyone begins to set up a list of boxes to check, you can be sure God is not real excited about it. If you get caught in the pit of religion, you'll be wondering your whole life if you are good enough.

Did I check enough boxes?

Did I serve on the right committees?

Did I go to the right building?

Did we use the right music?

Did I choose the right curriculum?

Did we do enough home quiet times?

Can we stand before God and be sure we did all we could to do more good than bad?

But if it's joy you're looking for, you start asking questions like:

How does that man feel about living on the street all alone?

What must it be like to live in a world filled with racism?

Did I make that guy feel important?

God, will You help me to see someone's needs today so I can meet them?

You see the difference?

One way of living forces you to wake up and check the list today; the other gives you a whole day to make up as you go.

I wonder which one Jesus decided to live by.

JOY

Joy is rest.

Joy is being with God and knowing Him.

Joy is God's knowing you intimately and passionately.

Joy is the sharing of feelings back and forth.

Joy is trust.

Joy is structure and spirit combining to form a wonderful life's orchestra so the whole world can hear how great God really is.

Joy is the foundation of relationships.

CHAPTER 12

PART OF A COMMUNITY

"LIVING IN COMMUNITY" is a popular phrase today in churches all over the world. We all want to live in some sort of community, but has anyone ever taken the time to think about the effort? Has anyone done a cost-benefit analysis for the sacrifice it takes to live in a community that knows each other and cares for one another?

Community isn't something you can just speak into existence. It takes work!

I'll explain.

When we first moved to Branson, Missouri, in 1997, Jamie and I looked for a church. It seemed as though for the first six months, we visited a new church almost weekly—and, believe me, there were plenty of options.

In a town with fewer than ten thousand people, there were more than eighty churches in the area. Think about that for a minute: If every person in the area decided to go to church, that's less than a thousand people at each location. And we know that every single person didn't go to church. So we found ourselves in services with five in attendance and services with a thousand.

Then one Sunday we were driving up north to Springfield at about noon and saw this beautiful building on the side of the road; it was a church. We thought if that many people were streaming out of the parking lot, there must be something exciting going on. We thought we'd give it a try. The next Sunday we walked into a building with four thousand people worshipping God, all at the same time. The energy was magnificent. I couldn't remember the last time I approached the throne of God with so much excitement, and that was something I surely wanted to hold on to.

We started going to the church every Sunday, and amazingly it was growing at breakneck speed. No one could have predicted that in the middle of Springfield, Missouri, there would be a church to boast of over ten thousand members. It just wasn't conceivable, but this church did it.

The worship style is still on the cusp of cultural awakening.

The preaching is one of the best teaching styles in the country.

The youth program is second to none (and I've been around a lot of youth programs in my days).

I just couldn't believe we stumbled onto something so great.

So I started asking myself, *How do they make this place so fun?*

How can a pastor develop a community so large and still not lose those of us who like to walk in the back and sit to spectate rather than participate?

KNOWING YOUR TRIBE

It sounds so simplistic, but it's true: Large groups are comprised of many smaller groups. Smaller groups are comprised of individuals who like to be around one another. So how do we go from the awful feeling of alone to actually connecting with the groups around us?

We've got to know who our tribe is.

One youth ministry invited me to be a consultant as they were trying to figure out how to connect young people on a weekly basis. Their youth group was exploding. At the time, they had more than five hundred kids in their youth group, so every time someone walked into the youth group, he got lost in the crowd.

Wouldn't you?

I don't know how you roll, but if there are a ton of people around and I don't know any of them, I tend to turn around and walk right back out.

And that's the key.

One-on-one, personal relationships are always the foundation to building a bigger group. I know that some of you are just longing for one friend to fill the hole in your heart right now, but I also know there are some of you who long to be in the middle of the social action. You'd like to be connected to a lot of people, but you just don't know how.

Get to know your tribe.

Each one of us functions inside a tribe of people, and we need to know who those people are.

Jocks.

Cheerleaders.

Goths.

Hipsters.

Hip-hop guys.

Those girls who just want boys to be around to give them attention.

Those boys who just want the girls to hang around to show how popular they can be.

The meatheads.

The fitness gurus.

The foodies.

The partiers.

And you can probably list another hundred categories.

I'm not trying to set stereotypes, but the fact is that we all run in certain circles. It doesn't mean you can't venture outside your circle or even run in multiple circles. But when tackling the problem of loneliness, seeking out a group of people with your same interests, passions, and abilities is an excellent starting point.

Now, the brilliant way to get close to folks is to set up a system for you to get to know them. I'm not advocating you join a group of people just because you want to be like them. Each one of us has been given a special gift from God, and we need to find the tribe or group of people where our gift most likely fits in the best.

If you're good at playing video games, you might spend a little time seeking out a tribe of people who do the same. Most likely it will happen naturally, but sometimes a jump start is necessary.

Once you've established who your tribe is, you can begin moving on to making relationship connections. For instance, the megachurch I was writing about decided to break down the masses into small groups. I think they called them "life groups," but essentially they were creating smaller communal tribes where people could actually share life together. It's sort of difficult to share life with ten thousand other people on a Sunday morning. In the same way, it's hard to make a real connection with your entire school, but you can introduce yourself to one person in one small tribe and start to make a real connection.

PARTICIPATING IN THE TRIBE

Look, you're never going to get over your loneliness feeling by yourself. It's not possible. Remember, you were made to exist with other people. Nobody on this planet was created to be a lone ranger; it's just not functional.

When I was in college, I took a psychology class dealing with the issues of non-connection. We read cases in which people were locked up in basements for *years* without any human physical contact, and the list of disorders filled a whole psychology book.

There is power when we connect with someone on a human level honestly and authentically. We begin making relational connections that propel the idea of the tribe to a group of people worth fighting for. After all, if you're just a spectator in your tribe, you might stand up for the people because they're cool, but if they let you down, they'll be yesterday's meatloaf, if you know what I mean.

So participation in the tribe is key.

If you're a jock and you like athletics, don't sit out. Push yourself to create life stories with other people. Of course, you never know what stories you'll be telling, because that's not how it works. Most of the best stories happen when the tribe gets together and something goes wrong. Together, they have to figure out how to get out of the situation and, in the process, they're bonded for life.

In 2002, my tribe was out doing a summer camping program in Durango, Colorado. We were making all kinds of stories together: bike rides, competitions, wakeboarding for the first time, finding the complete joy of biking on world-class mountain-biking trails.

One day I walked out of the dining hall and there were two-hundred-foot flames shooting off the tops of the pine trees on our mountain. We had three hundred people in camp at the time, and I'm telling you it was the scariest moment of my entire life.

There was an unusual forest-fire breakout that year, and the conditions were apparently just right for this fire to start consuming large portions of wilderness. We somehow evacuated all three hundred people from the camp in a little less than fourteen minutes. It was three weeks before the U.S. National Guard let us back in.

Mind you, I was hearing reports that the camp was all burned up, and I was fully prepared to walk out and find a new job. But when I turned the corner to enter the camp gates, I found all our buildings still standing. All the grass was green. All the flowers were growing. All the elements we used were still in place. There was a rubber mat that went up the mountain for kids to climb on, and no part of the rubber mat was melted even though the hillside was littered with burned timber.

I looked at my team in shock and awe.

We had a moment.

We knew in that very second that a miracle had occurred.

We knew that if God was willing to spare the camp, we had some unfinished business to take care of.

And worship we did.

Now, what kinds of bonds do you think were formed in our little tribe as the result of a natural disaster?

We weren't counting on it.

We weren't planning it.

But I can call any one of those team members for anything today and they'll be right at my side. That's how connection works. We must put ourselves in opportunities for experience and watch God begin the process of taking our loneliness away.

You can't sit in your room and pout because you don't have any friends. You've got to be assertive, get out there, and find some folks with common interests.

WHEN THE TRIBE GETS UGLY

The times I find people unwilling to engage, I hear them say things like, "Well, they just don't get me" or "I just don't fit in with that group," to which I say, *"So . . ."*

Again, forming a tribe means it will be comprised of people.

People have different personalities.

People like different things.

People bring baggage to their relationships, which complicates things.

We've got to learn how to deal with that.

Just because you're convinced that she talks too much and he smells like BO or her hair is the wrong color and he wears too many pairs of shorts, *who cares?*

I love the part of the Bible that talks about Jesus' role in coming to earth.

Remember?

"The Son of Man did not come to be served, but to serve" (Matthew 20:28).

Think about that for a second.

Jesus came to earth in the form of a baby in a manger. He took a life of poverty, or so it seemed. He hung out with several nomads. He lived in a dirty part of the world. And we are still talking about His impact on humanity.

He didn't come as a king.

He didn't come as a finance minister.

He didn't come as a power broker.

No, Jesus came to earth to serve mankind where *we* lived.

Jesus met us where we were instead of calling us to have to meet Him.

You see, the culture is interested in producing a consumer out of you. That's why all commercials exist.

"You'll look so much better if you use this brush on your hair."

"Your teeth will look so much whiter if you use this paste."

"You'll look like a model if you wear these boots."

"As long as it doesn't hurt anyone, you need this muscle enhancer."

It's so obvious.

But we've bought into it.

Our culture seriously thinks that if we buy the next gadget, people will think we're cool. Okay, if I drove a Ferrari down my street, I might get a few looks and a couple of whistles, but in the end, I would have just spent $400K on a car.

Do I really need the car?

Car and Driver says so.

My friends would think I was really cool. I might even have a different life if I got a chance to drive that car. But is anything *really* going to change?

I will tell you this: You'll never be able to connect with people because you bought something to impress them. You'll attract people around you, but loneliness will still be a part of your story. How do I know that?

How many pro-athletes are lonely after they retire? All the entourage wanted to see was money, power, and fame.

How many famous singers are sitting in lonely apartments trying for a comeback? All the buzz of the world left and they were left with who they are and the tribe they made.

Jesus came to earth and said, "If it's good enough for them, then it's good enough for me." He ate with His disciples, even though it was probably annoying sometimes. He slept around His disciples, even though someone probably didn't smell that great. He traveled with disciples, even though I'm sure some of them had to make more frequent rest stops than Jesus.

He lived *with* people, not *at* people.

And that's an integral part of the story.

You can't show up in fancy clothes and fast cars when trying to connect with a tribe of people who can barely afford to feed themselves and somehow think you're going to connect relationally. Sure, you can be seen as a savior of sorts to help them get out of the poverty they are living in, but in the end, a true friend is someone who knows you're in the relationship for much more than what *you* can get.

So when you're out there putting together your tribe, remember that if Jesus was humble enough to come to earth, surely there are some people in your life that you can put up with for the sake of building a tribe.

KNOWING WHO'S GOT YOUR BACK

And that's just it, right?

When someone can identify with you, stand in the loneliness with you, and find empathy, it works. Nobody wants someone who just lives in a constant state of patronization.

"Oh, you did sooo well in your game," she said, walking past, rolling her eyes.

Versus . . .

"I can't believe you! You're the most awesome basketball player I've ever seen," she said, putting her arm around her friend in celebration.

See the difference?

Authentic versus agenda-driven.

Caring for someone versus using someone.

When a tribe is built . . .

When experience glues relationships together . . .

When you can rest in the joy that a certain relationship gives you . . .

Loneliness starts to fade away.

But you can't do that on Facebook.

Twitter, Facebook, Google, and Skype are so much a part of our lives today. And that's okay. We can't just hide under a rock and pretend they're not there. They are important ways to connect.

But when social networking begins to replace the value of a true friend, you're living in an illusionary world. You may say, "I can experience things on Facebook I'd never experience with my friends in real life. We can post pictures, start group conversations, even record real-time videos." But let's be honest: Even if you got the chance to see the album of your friend visiting the most exotic part of the world, is it the same as you being there, seeing it with her?

And that's where I'm going here. If we can take the value of the social networking scene and combine it with real-time relationships, we might see this trend of loneliness take a positive direction.

What would life look like if we could really experience life together?

Community is important. To be able to contribute to the life of the community is even more fulfilling. Know your tribe, find a way to participate, and the result will be real-life friendships that last a lifetime.

CHAPTER 13

FULFILLMENT IN YOUR PURPOSE

AREN'T WE ALL just trying to figure out what we're doing here on the planet?

Ever looked up into the night sky and watched millions of heavenly stars and faraway planets?

Ever felt as though you were a small grain of sand on the big beach of life?

I've found myself looking up at the stars in a Colorado sky and just wondering what difference I make in the grand context of this world. And you know what? I know lots of people who think their lives are insignificant.

The drumbeat of life can drone out the spirit of adventure and allow the lonely feeling of solitude to wander in the longing spirit.

What are we doing?

Does my life really matter?

Is there something I'm supposed to be doing better than I'm doing it now?

How can what I do today really make a difference in the world?

I've sat with teenagers who feel as though they are insignificant.

I've sat with college students who ask every day, "Will it matter if I wake up tomorrow?"

I've talked with young professionals who sit in cubicles typing away for insurance companies, car dealerships, and finance firms who feel their lives are just a mirror of boredom.

So what's God's purpose for living a life full of sacrifice?

Does the Bible speak to a full, abundant life?

How can I know what God wants me to do?

CONFORMING OR TRANSFORMING?

Have you ever seen a beautiful painting hanging in the hallways of a famous art gallery? There are so many colors, so many textures, so many ways to create a beautiful impression. I've stood in front of one of those paintings with the apples in the bowl next to the flowers on the table, you know the ones. I thought for a second, *I wonder what this painting would look like if we took all the reds out of the picture.*

Can you imagine?

Have you ever been to a symphony and heard hundreds of instruments playing the same piece of art in unison?

I've listened to several city symphonies, and I often wonder, *What would this sound like if you took all the violins out of the room?*

Can you even imagine what that would sound like?

Life is incredibly similar.

Every one of us has a special color to share. We have a certain musical tone to add. Without our expression, life is a little less than it could be, but we've got to hone in and find out what part God has asked us to play.

Paul, the author of the majority of the New Testament, was a master of networking together people with different gifts. He understood that God's tapestry is made up of so many colors, shapes, and sizes. But before we can show people what our gifts are, we've got to step back and allow God to transform the way we see our gifts.

Romans 12 is one of my favorite chapters in the Bible, and it starts like this:

> I urge you, brothers and sisters, in view of God's mercy, to offer your bodies as a living sacrifice, holy and pleasing to God — this is your true and proper worship. Do not conform to the pattern of this world, but be transformed by the renewing of your mind. Then you will be able to test and approve what God's will is — his good, pleasing and perfect will. (verses 1-2)

The beauty of starting Romans 12 off with a couple of sacrificial verses is that Paul is actually allowing us a glimpse of the center of God's will. So many people are wandering through life thinking that God's will is something of a mystery, an abstract euphoric state of mind, when actually Paul invites us to know God's will through the transformation of our minds.

When we're trying to figure out our purpose in life under the banner of God's will in our lives, we've got to step back and ask, "What does it mean to conform?" and "What does it mean to transform?"

CONFORMATION

Nobody really likes the idea of being a conformist. No one likes to be called a copycat, a poser, or somebody who can't stand up for himself. But I know, there in the hallways of your high school or university, you can see people trying to look like their friends at every turn. It's quite amusing.

Jocks look like jocks.

Cheerleaders all look the same.

Goth kids have a special uniform they wear to school.

Musicians have a certain look about them.

Hipsters all wear low V-necks and black-rim glasses.

And every one of these groups has the impression they're all being individual in their own right. It's like watching a comedy of errors and the main characters have convinced themselves they're the different ones.

I can't talk too much, as I'm the same way.

The first time I went skiing in the mountains, I went to the ski rental store and asked the guy what kind of skis I needed. After I was all fitted for the hardware, it was time to check out the jackets, the pants, and the ski boots.

Fortunately (or unfortunately), at the time I had bought a bunch of clothes that were high energy, high color. That's what skiers wear, right? (Coloradans always make fun of skiers from other parts of the world. You can see them coming from a mile away with their big funny hats and neon clothes.)

So, off I went. For my first run on a real mountain, I was dressed like a neon sign.

As I got off the lift, I fell hard.

When I started to get up and try to ski, I couldn't stop; so when I got going too fast, I just fell over.

By the end of my first run, I was so frustrated. I remember thinking, *If this is what people do for fun, I'm out. I can just drink hot chocolate in the lodge all day and I'll be just fine.*

Before the end of the day, my friends urged me to give it one more go, and I agreed. So off we went, neon sign flashing.

But on this run, I noticed there were some other people going down the mountain on what looked like surfboards. They were gliding with the utmost ease. They had boots that seemed to be more comfortable than the solid plastic moon boots you have to wear to ski. They wore baggy clothes and cool helmets. They were the sign of individuality in the face of the ski conformity.

I decided I wanted to be one of them.

I marched back into the ski rental store to take back all my stuff and rent the snowboard gear. I was ecstatic as I thought about how I was getting ready to express myself as an individual, not taking the neon clothes as a thing of necessity. I was going to be my own man.

When I walked out of the shop with my baggy coat, baggy pants, cool boots, and the snowboard under my arm, I saw a group of snowboarders headed to the lift together. There were about eight of them all grouped up together, and in an instant I realized what I'd done.

They all had baggy coats.

They all had baggy pants.

They all had cool hats.

They all walked with a certain swag of individuality.

And I thought, *In my own search for individuality, I've become one of them. I am a part of the group. I'm a conformist!*

We all do it.

We watch commercials, sitcoms, and big-screen movies and we tend to curb our dress code around people we think are cool. For whatever reason, we're lining up to be just like everyone else.

It happens in high school.

It happens in college.

It happens in the workforce.

In fact, the only time I think it doesn't happen is when you're eighty years old and you don't care what people think about you anymore. (Ever spent time in the nursing home and dissected those conversations? *Yikes!* You can't get away with saying some of that stuff until you're at least sixty-five.)

TRANSFORMATION

This brings us to Paul's guarantee. If we can be transformed by the renewing of our minds, we can know what God's will is.

I've surveyed thousands of youth groups. I've spoken to hundreds of churches. I've listened to countless youth-director messages, and this concept of transformation has been hijacked.

Since the early days of youth ministry, for whatever reason, this concept of transformation has been sold to youth as a way to be different.

We've got to be weird for Jesus.

We've got to stand up in the face of our classmates.

"Make sure you wear your Christian T-shirt to set yourself apart and be transformed to God's will." Right?

And what have we done?

All our youth groups are the same. We have conformed!

They all look the same.

They all talk the same.

There's a strangeness about our Christian teenagers, and the world looks at us and calls us strange. Not "people who are interested in giving hope." No. Just plain weird.

Is that the nature of Christianity through the eyes of Paul?

Was he asking us to transform into some sort of weird state of cultural difference? Or was the "conform versus transform" conversation more to do with sin and the way the world tends to infuse our culture with sin so that we can't hear the will of God?

I'm convinced you can't hear the will of God unless you're able to clear your mind of the loudness of sin in the world.

Sin is all around us, right?

Everywhere we look, we're being tempted to lust, steal, lie, and live life differently than God asked us to live.

You have to be honest here.

And if you think for one second you're living in a world without temptation, then you've compromised the message of the Bible in its entirety. For it was Paul who said, "All have sinned and fall short of the glory of God" (Romans 3:23).

The Bible is the ultimate leveling field.

It doesn't matter if you're good at athletics.

It doesn't matter if you score the top grades in your school.

It doesn't matter if you've closed the biggest deal in the company.

We all have sinned, and that's where the transformation has to start. We have to look at the world as a place where we can transform from sinning and lusting to focusing on hope.

Sin is the culprit for loneliness.

Sin is the chief instigator of isolation.

Sin is the movement causing us to feel worthless.

Sin tells us we don't have a purpose, we don't have a gift, we don't belong to any certain group. And as sin drags us away from comfort and security, it begins to erode any sense of self-confidence we might have had.

Transformation doesn't mean you stand up in your classroom and be weird. How could you ever reach out and help someone if he or she thought you were a freak? Transformation by the renewing of your mind means to take captive the thoughts entering your conscious thought life.

Transformation means change from the world around you.

Transformation means seeing the world through His eyes.

And that brings us to you and your gifts.

THE BEAUTY OF THE PAINTING

> By the grace given me I say to every one of you: Do not think of yourself more highly than you ought, but rather think of yourself with sober judgment, in accordance with the faith God has distributed to each of you. (Romans 12:3)

I don't know any other section of Scripture more powerful in the lives of people who are feeling all alone. Look at God's beautiful design in the world and His intention to use each color of the human painting to make the most vibrant work of art in the universe.

HUMILITY

Let's not deceive ourselves.

Humility is something hard to come by. Nobody in the world finds humility an easy virtue to fall into. It takes work. It takes a conscious effort. It takes time. It takes discipline.

And it takes transformation.

You can't watch a football game today without watching the ultimate in hubris, arrogance, and conceited living. You don't have to be a student of football to see this go down. Just turn on the television on a Sunday afternoon during football season and watch for fifteen minutes.

Every play ends with a player throwing his arms in the air, doing a little dance in the end zone, or mocking the latest victim of his tackling dominance. The players act as though no one else in the world could have possibly played football as good as they did.

It's embarrassing.

I saw a commentator point this out in the 2011 football season. Bob Costas took some time during a Dallas Cowboy football halftime to look straight into the camera and invite the guys to just do their jobs. After all, they get paid millions of dollars; surely they could stop acting like idiots.

It's one thing to be confident; it's another thing altogether to see your confidence and make sure you use your gifts and talents in a humble way.

I don't know about you, but I'm intrigued every time I meet someone and it takes me a while to figure out what they do for a living. Have you ever done that?

Have you ever walked through an airport or seen someone in the shopping mall and you just knew he or she was someone special?

Not long ago, I met a pastor in the Northeast. He was talking about his understanding of apologetics, and because I've trained teens all over the world to understand the basic tenets of apologetics, we engaged.

He danced around some of the issues concerning moralism and epistemology, but there was something different about him.

He kept referring to his past life.

He mentioned he'd spent four years in a federal jail.

He talked about meeting celebrities in his former life.

And I just couldn't figure it out.

After our faith conversation, I started asking him, "What's the deal? What's all this about being in jail and seeing celebrities?"

Come to find out, this guy was a mastermind in the banking industry in the early 2000s. He claimed to have made millions of dollars in bank fraud before the 2008 market crash. He started naming celebrities he dated. He told me about the planes he owned. He talked a big game, how he was part of the banking elite for a short period of time.

"Why didn't you just come out and say it before?" I asked.

"It's just not a part of who I am anymore."

That's humility.

Here's a guy who knows he was a part of a life many people will only dream about or watch in the movies, yet he understands his role in life now. He doesn't think of himself as somebody special, and that quality endears him to others.

Have you ever felt like that?

You have a need down inside of you screaming to let people know all the good stuff you've done, but you're able to sit on it, be quiet, and allow someone else to get the glory?

The more time I spend with successful people, the more time I see the difference between cocky hubris and honest humility. Some people are just so insecure with who they are that they have to shout it from the mountaintop and pretend others care.

But some people have the sweet, strong conviction of their own value to the world, and it's those people who are the most influential in my life.

Take some time to think about your own approach to being known. Are you someone who has to inject your accomplishments into every conversation to garner love and adoration of those around you? Or can you take a step back and see the benefit of displaying your colors on the human painting when it's time and most needed?

THE COLORS OF THE PAINTING

> Just as each of us has one body with many members, and these members do not all have the same function, so in Christ we, though many, form one body, and each member belongs to all the others. We have different gifts, according to the grace given to each of us. If your gift is prophesying, then prophesy in accordance with your faith; if it is serving, then serve; if it is teaching, then teach; if it is to encourage, then give encouragement; if it is giving, then give generously; if it is to lead, do it diligently; if it is to show mercy, do it cheerfully. (Romans 12:4-8)

I've spoken to Christian groups all over the world.

I've seen Baptist churches, Bible churches, Pentecostal churches, Methodists, Presbyterians, Episcopalians, and Catholics.

I've participated in worship services of almost every flavor you can imagine. The one thing they all have in common is an underlying notion that their way of worship is the right way.

Of course it makes sense.

You wouldn't go to a place of worship if you thought for a second it could be the wrong way to approach God.

So I get it.

I know when I walk into an established community that they have reason to think their way is the best way.

But what would happen if we could step back and see the world the way God sees it?

Paul talks about the whole of the body, with many parts. Now, you have to take into account that there weren't as many denominational segments Paul was writing to in his day. There were certain people who taught different ways to approach God, but by no means was there the divisive nature of faith we have in our culture today.

I think Paul's intent here is right on.

He tells us there is one *big* body and there are several parts working in tandem with one another. They all function so the body can function as a whole. (Read also 1 Corinthians 12 for more insight on spiritual gifts.)

I think the spiritual-gift conversation has gone widely overlooked in some circles. There is a tendency for some denominations to overemphasize the power of spirituality, but there's also a minimalist approach to teaching people that they matter.

And remember, we're talking about the fundamentals to purpose. Why do we matter, and how can we be in a place of community rather than isolation?

Take the worship movement of the late 1990s to the present.

There's a subtle movement happening inside the walls of certain churches to elevate the purpose of a musician as a worship leader. When I was growing up in church, we had a piano on one side of the church and an organ on the other. Those have been replaced with full-on rock concerts with lights, smoke, and sound—the norm in the church today—rather than exploring reverent holy moments of worship.

Smaller churches call it "contemporary" service, while megachurches just call it "church."

There's nothing wrong with different styles of music.

There's nothing wrong with making worship something that is authentic, honest, and relevant to today's church and worshipping public. But there is something wrong when everyone in the church puts the rock-star worship leader up on an idolatrous platform and thinks somehow he or she has a closer "in" with God.

It's just not right.

In order to understand the "many parts and one body" principle, we have to approach our everyday worship lives with a sense of humility and honor. We should give encouragement to the worship leader taking us to the throne room of God, but we should also give similar encouragement to the volunteers in the nursery changing dirty diapers on Sunday morning.

Get it?

Let's think about ways this might play out in everyday life.

Some people just have the right stuff to do whatever they're doing.

Michael Jordan was born to play basketball.

Lance Armstrong was born to ride a bike.

Andrea Bocelli was born to sing.

Albert Einstein was born to think physics.

Peyton Manning was born to play football.

Billy Graham was born to preach.

It doesn't matter how hard you try to be one of the people on that list, you're never going to be them. God made them special. He gave them gifts to succeed in their various silos of life.

You'll never play basketball as good as Mike.

You'll never win as many Tour de France championships as Lance.

You'll never sing just like Bocelli.

And on and on and on.

But that's okay.

Part of understanding how to alleviate loneliness is finding a still confidence in our souls able to encourage people in their own giftedness and then turn around and find our own. Every person on this planet has been given the beautiful colors to make up God's ultimate painting. Every person has a specific gift only he or she can express. Nobody has them all. Nobody can do it just like anyone else. Everyone is individual. And that's what forces us to need every component we can.

If you can sing, sing with all your might.

If you can think, think as best you can.

If you're an athlete, you should play as though no one else can play like you.

If you're a teacher, you should teach with all that's inside you.

Why?

Because nobody can do it quite like you can.

Isn't that awesome?

If we can begin to share encouragement with those we know have certain gifts . . .

If we can humbly accept the fact that we have a different gift and it matters no matter what it is . . .

If we can get over the competitive nature of posturing to be on top . . .

If our goal can be to unify instead of isolate . . .

Then we can develop a community worthy of God's calling.

We can sit in the truth of Jesus' commandment: "Love one another. As I have loved you, so you must love one another. By this everyone will know that you are my disciples, if you love one another" (John 13:34-35).

And coincidently, Paul said something similar in Romans 12.

A COMMUNITY BUILT ON LOVE

> Love must be sincere. Hate what is evil; cling to what is good. Be devoted to one another in love. Honor one another above yourselves. Never be lacking in zeal, but keep your spiritual fervor, serving the Lord. Be joyful in hope, patient in affliction, faithful in prayer. Share with the Lord's people who are in need. Practice hospitality. (Romans 12:9-13)

Can you believe that?

Right after expressing the need for all the colors of God's tapestry to express themselves to the fullest while remaining steadfast in humility, Paul asks us all to reach out and love one another.

Some might say, "He's trying to encourage believers to love believers."

Read on . . .

> Bless those who persecute you; bless and do not curse. Rejoice with those who rejoice; mourn with those who mourn. Live in harmony with one another. Do not be proud, but be willing to associate with people of low position. Do not be conceited.
>
> Do not repay anyone evil for evil. Be careful to do what is right in the eyes of everyone. If it is possible, as far as it depends on you, live at peace with everyone. Do not take revenge, my dear friends, but leave room for God's wrath, for it is written: "It is mine to avenge; I will repay," says the Lord. On the contrary:
>
> "If your enemy is hungry, feed him;
> if he is thirsty, give him something to drink.
> In doing this, you will heap burning coals on his head."
>
> Do not be overcome by evil, but overcome evil with good. (verses 14-21)

The bottom line is, we need you.

We need you to express your gifts to the whole of humanity.

We need thinkers.

We need artists.

We need athletes.

We need teachers.

We need administrators.

We need servant hearts.

We need encouragers.

We need caregivers.

We need technical people.

We need visionaries.

We need all the people God created, with all the gifts He gave us, to make sure we see the abundant life God came to make.

If you truly desire to relieve yourself from the isolation you feel from day to day, get in a community.

Take some time to encourage people in their gifts, and by doing so you'll create trust. You'll find that trust begets trust, and soon the same people you're encouraging will give the same gift back to you. And in the end, we can sit with confidence in the beauty of God's design to make the world shout to the heavens, "The heavens declare the glory of God; the skies proclaim the work of his hands" (Psalm 19:1).

It's a testimony to God's creativity when you express your own individual gifts through the humility of knowing that God is the Creator and giver of all things.

CHAPTER 14

THE GAME CHANGER

Once you were alienated from God and were enemies in your minds because of your evil behavior. But now he has reconciled you by Christ's physical body through death to present you holy in his sight, without blemish and free from accusation.

— Colossians 1:21-22

THE NEED FOR VALIDATION

One of the pitfalls of loneliness is the feeling of insignificance. The whole of the human condition is walking through life trying to find someone, *anyone*, who will reach out and tell them, "You're worth it."

We try to find validation through fashion.

We try to find acceptance through behavior.

We associate ourselves with people who can bring a sense of belonging to our own world.

We even bend and change our moral convictions if we think there's a chance we might be thought of as normal.

It's who we are.

It's human.

And contrary to popular belief, the Bible isn't filled with perfect people following the perfect will of God. No, the Bible is filled with imperfect people God chooses to validate in spite of their afflictions.

God gave people such as Abraham, Jacob, Samson, Jonah, Peter, and Paul—despite their sins and shortcomings—purposes and roles in His ultimate plan for the world.

These are only a few.

If you take the long journey through the center of biblical character development, you'll find people who were just like you and me.

They wanted to be accepted.

They wanted their lives to matter.

They constantly were questioning whether God knew what He was doing.

They made mistakes.

They often ran from the obvious calling on their lives.

They were *human*!

And then Jesus the game changer came to create that one moment in the history of the universe where everyone stood up, in the muck and mire of their own loneliness, and cheered for God's blessing on them.

JESUS CAME TO BE A FRIEND

Jesus said, "I no longer call you servants, because a servant does not know his master's business. Instead, I have called you friends, for everything that I learned from my Father I have made known to you" (John 15:15).

Paul referred to Jesus as "the firstborn over all creation" (Colossians 1:15).

He claimed Jesus to be the reason for all things to be, both in heaven and earth.

He helped frame the divinity of Jesus in the first section of Colossians so well that it's hard to mistake the importance Jesus has to the whole world.

If you take time to read through the Gospels, you find the beginning of the game-changer message. The disciple named John traveled with Jesus, and many have written of Jesus' affinity for his closest friend. Peter, James, and John were all considered to be in the closest of circles with Jesus throughout His time here on earth.

John writes one of the most prolific scenes in his gospel in chapter 15. Jesus was dining on one of the last meals He'd have together with the disciples and began to lay out the events of the coming days for them. When Jesus turned to them and said, "I no longer call you servants. . . . Instead, I have called you friends" (verse 15), the whole universe must have jumped up in recognition of the change in the game. This was the first time any being considered to be the creator of all things had mentioned humankind rallying around some sort of friendship-type relationship.

No other religion makes the same claim.

No other god visited the world to become friends with mankind.

The stories of all other religions are centered around the need for mankind to fit into the ideal world created by the god.

In ancient days, people had to please the gods with sacrifices.

If the moon god was mad, there had to be certain requirements fulfilled to appease him.

If the sea god was angry, the population spent much of their time trying to figure out how to redeem his good will.

But here in John 15, there is a divine person sitting at a dining table with His fellow humans, and He is declaring a friendship with mankind.

Do you know how huge that is?

Imagine your celebrity hero coming over to your house, sitting at your dining table, and revealing the desire to befriend you. Would you be excited? Now multiply that feeling by, say, oh, the *Creator of all things*!

He made the planets spin in the universe.

He hurled the stars into the sky.

He knows the number of hairs on your head.

He knows how many days you're going to live.

He knows what's going to happen today, tomorrow, and for all time.

He created it.

And He—*that guy*—wants to be your friend?

As my good friend from the South used to say, "That's crazy talk right there."

Jesus' desire for friendship changes *everything*. He didn't come and demand that you form to His way. He didn't come in anger to regulate sin. He didn't even come to the earth in the form of the King He is.

He came humbly to present the best way of living life as He created it, and no other deity in the history of faith in the world has ever come to extend its hand of sovereignty to mankind. It's absolutely unique.

THE INFLUENCE OF JESUS

The stretch of Jesus' influence can't be overstated.

As Paul pointed out in Colossians, He is the Creator of all things and in Him all things hold together.

When John wrote his revelations at the end of the Bible, he was sure to include this statement made by Jesus in His overall vision: "I am the Alpha and the Omega . . . who is, and who was, and who is to come, the Almighty" (Revelation 1:8).

Alpha is the first letter in the Greek alphabet. Omega is the last. Jesus was making a declaration of comprehension. He revealed Himself to be before all things, at the end of all things, and ultimately a part of everything in the middle. His expanse of unity in the heart of mankind is all-encompassing.

Why does that matter?

Because in the end, when we feel the loneliest . . .

When we feel as though no one cares . . .

When we feel lost in our own spheres of influence . . .

When we can't find anyone in the world willing to share his or her care with us . . .

You've got to know that the message of Jesus isn't just saying a prayer and living a good life. His involvement in the world today spans all things.

THE HIJACKING OF JESUS

For whatever reason, there's some sort of instant Christianity sweeping across America. You know what I mean? It's the message that if you can give your life over to Jesus, invite Him into your heart, sign a card at the front of the church, and begin attending the service every Sunday, then somehow your life is going to be miraculously different.

I will stand witness to my dying day, *that's not in the Bible!*

Sure, there are subtle verses that lead someone to that conclusion. Traditional values are certainly a part of a conservative culture. But in the end, there's no simple way to get enough of Jesus where you can just check a box, make a list, or live inside a boundary of rules and regulations in order to feel satisfied that Jesus is with you.

I believe that people have hijacked the freedom Jesus came to give us.

We don't have to rely on someone to lead us to God.

We don't have to attend a service for God to smile down on us.

We don't even have to give a dime for God to welcome us into His family.

No.

The love of God spans all time.

It covers all sin.

It gives us hope in those times when we feel as if there's nothing else to give us hope.

It helps us to know that ultimately all the evil in the world will be reconciled by a Judge.

Jesus is the key! He's not the first step in a recovery plan; He *is* the recovery plan. He's not the bridge to get you to a better place; He *is* the better place. He's not a genie in a bottle that you can call on when life seems unmanageable; He *is* life.

If you had a celebrity idol pull you out of the crowd and put you on display as his or her friend, you'd feel like a million bucks. You'd have a sense about you that somewhere in the world, you mattered. You'd be able to post those pictures on Facebook and tell all your friends you just met the coolest person in the world.

How much more are you able to live fulfilled knowing that the Creator of the universe wants to hang out with you?

He wants to spend time with you.

He wants to know you.

He wants you to know Him.

The Bible says, "Here I am! I stand at the door and knock. If anyone hears my voice and opens the door, I will come in and eat with that person, and they with me" (Revelation 3:20).

The message of Jesus isn't simply to make your life wonderful, clean, and void of hardship; the message of Jesus is that the Creator of the universe came to earth to begin a relationship with you.

And guess what? He's not leaving.

NEVER ALONE

So many of our friendships in this world end in pain.

People let us down. We expect they will be loyal. We count on people to do what they say. We think commitments are forever. And if you're anything like me, when someone shows signs of making a mockery of my friendship, I often run away.

I run away in disgust. I run away because I can't trust the person anymore. I run away because I thought life was going to be one way but in reality it turned out differently than I thought.

Have you ever been there?

Have you ever been let down?

Maybe you experienced the tragedy of divorce in your own family. Maybe you felt the sting of rejection when a friend ratted you out. Maybe you had a moment when your whole world came crashing down and all the people you thought were going to support you turned their backs on you.

The beauty of Jesus' message is that He will never leave you.

He didn't leave Jacob (see Genesis 28:15).

He didn't leave Moses or Joshua (see Joshua 1:5).

He didn't leave the Israelites (see 1 Samuel 12:22).

He didn't leave Ezra (see Ezra 9:9).

He didn't leave Nehemiah (see Nehemiah 9:31).

He didn't leave David (see Psalm 9:10).

He didn't leave the poor (see Isaiah 41:17).

He didn't leave the disciples (see Matthew 28:20).

And He promises not to leave the people who worship Him (see Hebrews 13:5).

It doesn't mean there won't be times when God seems quiet.

It doesn't mean that every day of your life is going to be filled with the feeling of togetherness.

In fact, some of the greatest men and women of the faith who have walked through this earth found extreme solitude.

But it does mean that the Creator of the universe made a promise throughout history to be with us. He promised never to leave me stranded to myself. He gives me hope that someday He'll return and everything I know to be true about feeling alone will disappear to history and forever there will be some sort of union . . . Emmanuel . . . God with us.

When I feel that no one gets me . . .

When I feel as though there's no one around to care for me . . .

When I feel afraid to reach out to someone else . . .

When I struggle to know what my gifts and purpose are . . .

When I can't seem to relate to the other people in my tribe . . .

When I feel boxed in by labels that just don't fit . . .

When I feel as though life is filled with the pit of loneliness, I find comfort knowing that God will stand with me to the end of the world.

With Him, I am never alone.

NOTES

Chapter 2: The Online Connection

1. Facebook Newsroom, "Statistics," http://newsroom.fb.com/content/default.aspx?NewsAreaId=22.

Chapter 3: One Body, Different Gifts

1. Daniel J. DeNoon, "Speech Anxiety Worse for Some, but Most Can Overcome It," *WebMD.com,* April 20, 2006, http://www.webmd.com/anxiety-panic/guide/20061101/fear-public-speaking.

Chapter 4: Walking in the Darkness

1. Teen Depression, "Teenage Depression Statistics," http://www.teendepression.org/stats/teenage-depression-statistics/.
2. Teen Depression, "Teenage Depression Statistics," http://www.teendepression.org/stats/teenage-depression-statistics/.

Chapter 5: Nobody Cares

1. American Academy of Child & Adolescent Psychiatry, "Teen Suicide," aacap.org, May 2008, http://www.aacap.org/cs/root/facts_for_families/teen_suicide.

Chapter 6: Core Fears

1. "Farley died from overdose of cocaine, morphine," CNN Interactive, January 2, 1998, http://www.cnn.com/SHOWBIZ/9801/02/farley.autopsy/.

Chapter 7: Addictions

1. Steven Tyler, *Does the Noise in My Head Bother You? A Rock 'n' Roll Memoir* (New York: HarperLuxe, 2011).
2. Jerry Ropelato, "Internet Pornography Statistics," toptenreviews.com, http://internet-filter-review.toptenreviews.com/internet-pornography-statistics.html.

Chapter 8: Looking for Love in All the Wrong Places

1. National Association for Shoplifting Prevention, "Shoplifting Statistics," shopliftingprevention.org, http://www.shopliftingprevention.org/whatnaspoffers/nrc/publiceducstats.htm.

Chapter 11: Real Joy

1. Merriam-Webster, "bestow," m-w.com, http://www.merriam-webster.com/dictionary/bestow.

ABOUT THE AUTHOR

ANDY BRANER is an ordained minister and the former president of Kanakuk Colorado Kamp in Bayfield, Colorado. His mission is to create a place where teenagers can explore their faith and understand the Christian worldview and to provide opportunities for teenagers to engage in God's work around the world.

Andy recently started a nonprofit camping ministry called Ahava ministries. The first location is KIVU (www.campkivu.com), where a team of college students provides Christian worldview training to teenagers for fourteen days a term each summer. Andy teaches Christian worldview classes to approximately a thousand teenagers and three hundred college-age counselors each summer. His desire is to teach young people what it means to be "Realife/Realfaith" followers of Jesus.

KIVU has started a gap-year program for high school students to take a year between graduation and their freshman year of college. This program is proving to be a wonderful opportunity for students to explore issues such as poverty and God's view of the poor, international business, and global relationships with different countries. You can learn more about the gap year at www.kivugapyear.com.

In an average year, Andy speaks to more than 80,000 high school and college students in both public and private schools. He teaches on a wide variety of topics, including Christian worldview, basic apologetics, sexuality, culture, Christians in the arts and entertainment, and world religions. He frequently speaks at youth conferences, churches, schools, and universities.

Andy lives with his wife and five children in Durango, Colorado, where they continue to seek God's will for their family.